THE BOXCAR

MILLIONAIRE

TOM BLACK'S PROVEN SYSTEM OF SALES SUCCESS

Editor-in Chief: Jennifer K. Lill
Design Manager: iDesign Inc.
Interior and Cover Design: Brian Hamblen
Illustrations: Bryce Damuth
Technical Consultants: Anthony Davis, Brian Hamblen, Steven Boone,
Matt Cramer
Printer: Lithographics Inc.

ISBN: 0-9792423-0-4

To order additional copies write, fax, or visit our website: tomblackcenter.com

Tom Black Center for Selling, Inc.

6204 Harding Pike
Nashville, TN 37205
615.477.7125 (wk)
615.833.1889 (fax)

www.tomblackcenter.com

This book is dedicated to:

Sam Johnson

my former sales manager and mentor.

Special thanks go to the following people:

My Parents

Bill King

Don Napier

Walt Wasyliw

Steve Counts

Dale Loftus

James Wedgeworth

David Vandewater

Roy Loftin

Greg Daily

Jennifer Lill

TABLE OF CONTENTS

*"No one can stop you from succeeding
without your permission."*

INTRODUCTION

THE BOXCAR MILLIONAIRE

We all have a story, don't we? We encounter circumstances in life – things that we either overcome or they overcome us.

As for Tom's story, it is the quintessential "rags to riches" tale, a narrative that embodies the American Dream. It brings truth to the cliché that what you can dream, you can achieve.

> *"For the first few years of his life he lived with his family in a railroad boxcar..."*

Tom was born in the small town of Nickerson, Kansas, and for the first few years of his life lived with his family in a railroad boxcar – a boxcar. It was set off the tracks and divided into two bedrooms and one living space. The bathroom was outside. His mother tried with what little they had to make it seem like something else, but it was undeniably a boxcar. Cockroaches were a way of life for Tom, no matter how hard they tried to get rid of them.

Neither parent finished high school and the family struggled for necessities. The Black family moved into an old two-bedroom house where Tom shared a room with his sister. The house had one tiny bathroom and one gas stove for heat. Tom's clothes were hand-me-downs; as the youngest child, the term "new" was non-existent.

The funny thing is, Tom never realized he was one of the poor kids until one day in seventh grade when some of his classmates were making fun of his clothes. He was never embarrassed of where he came from. In fact, he embraces his beginnings. From that moment on, however, he realized one thing: He never wanted to be poor again, he never wanted to wonder if he'd have ever have new clothes to wear, and he wanted to taste what "significant" was. He wanted a better life.

So, he began to picture it … he began to dream about it … he began to live it in his mind. Then, he began to make his own way to the place where one day his dreams would be reality. Tom sold candy in the Boy Scouts and he was good at it. He loved the satisfaction of hearing that "yes" from customers. He loved the sound of that word – YES! He tried his hand at selling anything that could make an extra dollar – he tried to sell seeds, potholders, and Amway, but quite frankly, Tom failed at selling those things.

That didn't discourage him. By that point, he'd heard it all: Tom, you've got too much working against you. Tom, your family is poor. Tom, you can never afford college.

And they were right; he didn't have the money. That was reality. But here's another reality – one September day, he walked into his first college classroom. No one was going to make Tom feel inferior without his permission.

Tom was the first in his family to attend college. On a day he will never forget, a man who would change the course of his life approached him. He was a recruiter for the Southwestern Company out of Nashville, Tennessee. He had no idea at that moment what he had stumbled upon. The Southwestern Company recruits thousands of college students each summer to sell books door-to-door – to make money, and to change their lives and attitudes toward hard work.

Do not be mistaken: There was nothing glamorous about it. It is cold-calling in a strange place far away from home. It is strangers, sweat, rain, 80-plus hour work-weeks, rejection, discouragement, attack dogs, homesickness. Tom left college for the summer with $50 in his pocket and went to Nashville to learn how to sell on a straight commission basis. He paid his own expenses.

> *"This was Tom's turning point – a time every great man or woman has to come to in order to break through from good to great..."*

This was Tom's turning point – a time every great man or woman has to come to in order to break through from good to great, from surviving to thriving. Before the summer ended, it would become part of the foundation that makes him who he is today. His turning point came when he realized that all he needed was a chance, the chance to stand out above the crowd. That is all many of us ever need, that turning point, that chance to turn your career or your life around.

This book could be your chance to do just that. You can take your selling career from good to great and become as successful as you make up your mind to be.

So let's go back to that first summer. The company puts its recruits through intense sales training and sends them hundreds of miles from home to run their own businesses for the summer months. With no money, no car, and paying his own expenses, Tom had nothing to thrust him into success but sheer determination.

This boxcar kid was gonna be somebody. He knew if he failed, he would have no one to blame but himself. Win or lose, ultimately it was up to Tom. So, he bought a used bike from a customer and started knocking. He rode and he knocked. If he heard "no", he would jump back on that bike and he would ride, and he would knock.

Tom was taken down to the police station seven times that first summer in Bowling Green, Kentucky. They would demand to see his selling permit, harass him, and leave him at the police station with no way to get back to his sales territory.

Without a car, Tom had to be dropped off in his territory each morning to pick up his bike and start selling. His roommate who had a car was supposed to come back each night at 9:30 p.m. and pick Tom up. One day, he was dropped off as usual, but later learned that his roommate had quit and gone home. Tom waited at the pick-up spot, not realizing what had happened, and finally started walking back. That night, tired and exhausted, Tom slept in an old barn beside the highway. He woke up in the morning, hitchhiked his way back into town, picked up his bike, and started knocking again at 8 a.m.

With all the obstacles, did Tom fail that summer on the "bookfield", the term affectionately used to refer to the students' sales territories? No, he did not fail – in fact, he ranked eighth in the company that summer. And for three summers, he ranked number one. He broke several sales records and continued to outdo his personal bests every summer.

He was asked to work full-time as a sales manager for the company. His teams went on to shatter company team records because of his teaching and coaching. And you know what? This small-town Kansas kid built a legacy for himself there. His techniques are still taught at The Southwestern Company today, more than 30 years later.

During five summers on the bookfield, he had heard more "no's" than most people hear in a lifetime. He had also heard more "yes's" than most salespeople will hear in their careers. His summers were full of sweat, toil, more sweat – and, ultimately, incredible success.

His post-Southwestern career began as the sales manager for Windsor Publishing Company, a publisher of civic guides in California. He quickly rose to become National Sales Manager and made a name for himself by introducing several new products that were highly successful for the company. While there, he personally recruited and trained more than 200 commission salespeople.

His sales management techniques and success were becoming common knowledge in the corporate arena. He was soon recruited to join Madison Financial, a corporation specializing in retail marketing strategies designed for banks. CUC International soon absorbed Madison Financial. CUC then acquired Benefit Consultants, and Tom spearheaded the growth of the sales division and did what no one in the company thought was possible. Under his leadership, sales skyrocketed from $10 million to more than $350 million in a matter of a few years. That same motivation, that same desire of his youth never left him and Tom knew no one could ever discourage him without his permission.

This was the start of a new direction in his journey; he became an innovative leader in the banking industry. He then started Private Business, Inc., a company that pioneers accounts receivable lending for banks. Under his six-year leadership as CEO, Private Business, Inc. grew into the country's leading provider of accounts receivable programs for community banks and their commercial customers. He grew the sales force from non-existent to over a hundred salespeople strong. The company went public in May 1999.

In January 1999, he and a partner purchased Tecniflex, Inc. and formed Imagic Corporation as a sister company. Tecniflex, Inc. sells mission-critical equipment and ATMs and provides hardware maintenance to banks nationwide. He created Imagic Corporation to develop check-imaging systems.

As CEO of both Tecniflex and Imagic, he expanded both companies from small regional providers to national sales and service organizations. Under his leadership, Tecniflex went from an insignificant regional company to a national company serving 4,000 banks in 49 states. Tom achieved this by doing what he'd come to do best – producing world-class salespeople through a proven sales success system.

In December 2001, Imagic Corporation merged with Open Solutions, Inc. Open Solutions then went public, marking Tom's second public company.

Today, this small town boxcar kid lives in Nashville, Tennessee on his plantation estate, where he has the opportunity to devote time, money, and efforts to countless charities and causes.

He is one of America's largest and most recognized wine collectors. He counts the world's greatest winemakers, chefs, and wine critics among his closest friends. He has conducted some of the most comprehensive and famous wine-tastings in America. His personal wine collection has nearly 30,000 bottles, and he owns some of the rarest wines in the world.

You know about Tom's turning point. Now it is time you find your own. Maybe your turning point will come when you read how simple it is to do unforgettable follow-up calls. Maybe it will come when you know how to set smart goals that achieve results. Maybe the light will go on when you read how to close stronger and more often. But this much is true: You owe it to yourself to find that point, that sentence, that chapter, or even that one technique that will break you through to the next level in your career.

We all want to be great, to provide for our families, and to make a difference with our lives. No one believed this small-town poor kid would amount to anything. But what you must never forget is no one can stop you from succeeding without your permission. Tom Black has proven to even the greatest of skeptics that you don't have to be a natural-born salesperson, or born into money, or even be the sharpest dressed to achieve greatness in your career. He did it in khaki pants and a cowboy hat knocking on doors in the hot summer sun. He changed the lives of countless families with his products. But as much as he helped these families, they helped Tom so much more than they'll ever know.

Now it is his turn to pass it along, to share his training methods and proven business models with you. But you can't just dream big. You have to think big, and then plan big, just as Tom did. We are all capable of finding our turning point. It is not some mythical destination. You can achieve genuine sales success, find your turning point and sell more than you ever thought was possible.

"Successful people form the habit of doing the things unsuccessful people don't want to do or know how to do."

Chapter 1

The "Three Little Determinants" of Sales Success

You Aren't Going to Believe This

A man came home from work early and found a cigar burning in the ashtray. He immediately thought his wife had been seeing another man. He looked all over the apartment and could not find him. He ran out on the balcony and there, four floors below, was a man straightening his tie.

"That's the guy!" he thought to himself.

Filled with rage, he ran back into the kitchen, grabbed the refrigerator, dropped it on the man and smashed him flat. But he so over-exerted himself in the process that he died right there of a heart attack.

The scene changes – now a man is standing in line with several others at Heaven's gate to see St. Peter. St. Peter turns and asks the first man in line, "So how did you die?"

"You aren't going to believe this," said the first man, "but I was standing in front of a building straightening my tie, and a refrigerator fell out of nowhere and smashed me flat."

"Come on in," replied St. Peter.

"I'd like to get into heaven too," says the next man in line.

"So how did you die?" asked St. Peter.

"You aren't going to believe this," said the second man, "but I was moving this refrigerator around, over-exerted myself, and died of a heart attack."

"Come on in," says St. Peter.

A third man walks up to St. Peter. "I just died and I'd like to get into heaven," he said.

St. Peter asks the man, "And how did you die?"

"You aren't going to believe this," responded the third man, "but I was sitting in this refrigerator…"

Did you have to think about that one for a minute? The point is this: "You aren't going to believe this," but success in selling is dependent on three things and only three things. The purpose of this book is to thoroughly discuss these elements of selling.

> *"…success in selling is dependent on three things and only three things."*

Let's Start With a Definition of Selling

The fundamental definition of selling is this: Sales is a transference of feeling about a product or idea. Another way to look at sales is like this – the primary and simplified purpose of the sales process is to bring a prospect to a point of decision. That decision may be yes, no, or maybe, but the sales process doesn't occur without this element – the point of decision.

Also inherent in the sales process is finding or creating a need for a wanted or needed service or product. Sometimes this is intentionally done by the salesperson, sometimes it isn't. Regardless, this is part of the process.

Here is a story that illustrates this definition of selling. Charlie was a tongue-tied accountant who worked for a toothbrush company. He noticed that the salespeople in his company were making more money than he, so he went to the sales manager to ask for a job.

The sales manager discouraged him because of his speech problems and complete lack of experience. But Charlie persisted, and the sales manager decided to give him a try.

"Here are 100 toothbrushes," the sales manager told Charlie. "Now go see what you can do."

The next day, Charlie came back reporting that he had sold them all. The sales manager gave him 200 more toothbrushes that day, and sure enough, the next day Charlie had sold them all.

The sales manager said, "Well Charlie, you've got yourself a job. By the way, how did you sell so many toothbrushes?"

"Oh, it was pretty simple, really," said Charlie. "I went to the busiest corner in town and put up a booth with a sign that said 'Free Brownies.' Everybody loves brownies. When they walked by, I'd say, 'Do you want a free brownie' and everybody took one. When they bit into the brownie, they'd exclaim, 'It tastes like crap!'

"And I'd say, 'It is crap! You wanna buy a toothbrush?'"

Charlie did it all. He created a need, presented a product, and he brought potential buyers to a point of decision. Selling is all of those things.

Success for Rent

How about success? Earl Nightingale said, "Success is the progressive realization of a worthwhile goal or dream." That's a good definition. I'll take that a step further by adding that success is not something you own . . . it is something you rent. It is progressive. The rent is due every day, and when you stop paying the rent on success, you start paying the rent on failure.

Yesterday's successes lull us into today's complacencies, which lead to tomorrow's failures. If you ask a hundred new salespeople if they want to be successful, they will all say yes. They will all have different definitions of success, but they all want it. On the other hand, if you asked a hundred new salespeople if they wanted to be failures, I doubt anyone would sign up for that program.

However, there is a common denominator of success: Successful people form the habit of doing the things unsuccessful people don't want to do or know how to do.

Every successful person makes choices to do the things that unsuccessful people won't. It typically starts in school. Do you study and do your homework or do you watch TV? If you make the choice to study for the big exam rather than watch the big game, for the rest of your life you are likely saying "no" to immediate pleasures to achieve more pleasing end results. Successful people say "no" because there is "a bigger yes burning inside."

Henry Kissinger said, "Each success only buys an admission ticket to a more difficult problem."

Bill Russell, legendary NBA player and coach, had this to say on striving for success: "Getting to be number one is easy. You come on at 6-foot-10, have a good set of hands, have a great team. Staying there is hard. Every night some hot young player comes to test your hand. He's watching your films, he knows you better than you know yourself. Your only hope is to work harder, think smarter, and use your strengths."

> *"Successful people do the things that*
> *unsuccessful people simply don't do."*

First Things First

I am going to make a few assumptions here. I'm going to assume that you have a good product, a respectable company, and competitive pricing. If you don't have these things, find another position with a company that offers you these essential ingredients. All the great sales advice in the world won't serve any purpose if you sell a product you do not believe in, a product that is outrageously priced, or if you work for a company you do not respect.

These factors – a good company, a good product, and competitive pricing – are the racehorse that the sales jockey rides. Even the greatest jockey in the world won't win a race if he's on a bad horse. A good jockey can make a horse better, but let's face it, some horses were never born with the ability to win. There are countless numbers of good salespeople with real talent who will never be very successful purely because they make some bad choices in employers.

The "Trifecta" of Sales Success

Go find a good horse. Then, if you're a good jockey, you'll be off to the races. In order to get you ready, let's get back to those three little things that determine success in selling:

1. The number of prospects you see
2. The quality of your prospects
3. The quality of your presentation

Isn't that simple? Now I am going to spend the next 172 pages explaining how these three tickets to sales success are not quite as simplistic as they sound, but they are very attainable. I'll show you how.

You know, things are always better in three's...

In Review

- Success in selling is dependent on three things and only three things: The number of prospects you see, the quality of your prospects, and the quality of your presentation

- Sales is a transference of feeling about a product or idea.

- The primary purpose of the sales process is to bring a prospect to a point of decision.

- The rent on success is due every day, and when you stop paying the rent on success, you start paying the rent on failure.

- Successful people form the habit of doing the things unsuccessful people don't want to do or know how to do.

- Before a single sales technique is taught, it is critical to have these three things:

  1. A good company
  2. A good product
  3. Competitive pricing

Chapter

See More, Sell More

Movie sagas seem to come in threes. Three *Star Wars* (the originals anyway), *The Godfather* Trilogy, and don't forget *The Three Amigos* and *The Three Musketeers*. It seems like good things don't come in pairs; they come in threes. So, too, with selling and the three determinants of sales success.

Part One of the "Sales Saga"

Let's get right into the first determinant – the number of prospects you see. Successful salespeople believe in the law of averages. There is simply no such thing as luck in long-term selling success. It would be impossible for anyone to believe that the gas and oil that drive the free market enterprise is based on luck. Nothing happens until someone sells something. To believe that our economy is based on luck is too much to ask of any rational person. Selling is the real fuel that drives our economy.

The first principle of that belief in the free market enterprise is that the number of people you see, to a great extent, controls the number of people you sell. Life insurance companies form and thrive based on the principle that man, as an individual, is unpredictable, but that man, as a whole, is actually very predictable and follows the same recurring patterns of behavior.

> *"...two brothers follow each other everywhere: "See More" and "Sell More." Make them your new sales partners."*

A given number of 40-year-olds will die within a specific and measurable time frame if the test group is large enough. Which ones die? No one knows that. But that a certain number or percentage of them will die is a certainty. Advertising companies, TV stations, and Internet companies all charge for ad space and time depending upon the number of impressions. The underlying principle is the more you see, the more you sell. Think about it this way – two brothers follow each other everywhere: "See More" and "Sell More." Make them your new sales partners.

I Don't Like Excuses

Over the years as a sales manager, I have asked countless salespeople to change one little thing: See more people. I've heard excuses you haven't even thought of. Don't get any ideas, but here are some of my favorites:

- I'm trying to save the company money on my travel budget.
- My credit card is maxed.
- I have too much vacation time building up and I need to take some of my vacation days.
- I've seen everyone in my territory.
- I'm seeing as many as possible now. I'm simply out of time.
- I believe in quality not quantity.
- I want to spend more time with my best customers.
- I only want to see the right people.
- My approach doesn't work.
- Everyone in my territory has bought.
- Blah, blah, blah

There are two kinds of salespeople: Those who look for a way and those who look for an excuse. Successful salespeople go over, under, around, and through any obstacle to get the job done. If this standard is too hard for you, your calling may not be the sales profession, and you might want to consider a career change if this mindset is not to your liking. But if you're already in sales and you want a raise, just look in the mirror and give yourself one by committing to seeing more people.

Great companies built on great salespeople find a way, not an excuse. We've all heard the old adage that there are only three kinds of people: Those who make things happen, those who watch things happen, and those who say, "what happened." The world doesn't care about the storms you encounter; they only want to know if you brought in the ship.

There Are No Excuses

What did I tell those salespeople who gave me those excuses? First, I assured them that there are no valid excuses. Then I told them this: "Despite your objections, you can see more people."

I then showed them how to construct a plan of action that made further excuse making impossible – excuses can't compete with cold hard numbers and an action plan.

Here is the simple exercise I've taught over the years: Take the top two salespeople in your organization in number of presentations per week or month. Assuming you're not one of those two top performers, compare those numbers to what you are doing. For example, Morgan sees 10 prospects per week, Jennifer sees 9 per week, and you see 8 per week. By comparing yourself to the top performers in the company, this tells you what is possible in terms of your own activity.

Don't worry about the results of these two top performers in regard to sales. The focus in this exercise is on activity. More activity at your current performance level will naturally lead to more sales.

Hey, are you just gonna sit there or what?

Think about it this way: Every time a .300 hitter in baseball has ten at-bats, he gets three hits. If you increase his number of at-bats, he will still only get three hits every ten times he bats. So, even though his average number of hits won't change, he'll still be a .300 hitter. His number of hits will improve simply by increasing his number of at-bats.

The law of averages also doesn't care about strikeouts. After all, the great Babe Ruth held the record for strikeouts and homeruns simultaneously. Do people focus on his strikeouts when they mention Babe?

Goals: An Excuse's Worst Enemy

Now that you have a base line for what's best is your organization – the average number of presentations for the top two people in your company – you must now set a goal to increase your own number of presentations. Goal-setting is comprised of some very fundamental elements. We're going to get back to increasing your number of presentations, but an inherent part of increasing your numbers is a clear understanding of goals and how to set them.

Goals can be tricky, but they are also essential. They are especially critical in the world of selling. Salespeople have much more autonomy than do most professionals. Many of us have the luxury of making our own schedule, but this can become either a blessing or a curse.

> *"A salesperson without a goal is like a ship without a rudder."*

If you set goals with your time, this freedom can be a blessing. But without goals, you may end up like my first sales manager at the Southwestern Company used to say, "A salesperson without a goal is like a ship without a rudder." You don't want to spend your entire career straying off course.

I've never seen a successful company that didn't have an annual budget. That is a goal. While it's true that 10 different people may give you 10 different versions of what constitutes good goal-setting, what is fundamentally important is that you do set them. As Yogi Bera said, "You gotta have a goal or you might end up somewhere else."

Here are four elements to setting smart goals that will keep you on course:

I. Write it Down. The first element to good goal setting is to write it down. If you don't write it down, then it isn't a goal; it's a dream, a wish, a hope, but it's not a goal. Take out a piece of paper and write down the number of new presentations you want to make each week.

II. Set a Time Frame. The second element to good goal setting is to set a time frame. Say to yourself, "I will average nine presentations per week over the next three months or quarter." A time frame allows you to succeed or fail. Without a time frame, there is no success or failure; there is only constant reaching.

III. Tell Someone. The third element to good goal setting is to tell someone important to you about your goal. It could be your boss, spouse, parents, a peer, or a friend. The point is to put yourself on the line with someone who is important to you and who you respect.

Dizzy Dean was an amazing baseball pitcher in the 1940s. He told everyone that he and Paul Dean, his brother, were going to win 40 games the next baseball season. The next season they did something no one else had ever done – two brothers won 44 games for the same team. Dizzy told everyone his goal before the season to put pressure on himself and his brother to deliver. And they did.

After the season, Dizzy was on a bus, and a native St. Louis woman said, "Mr. Dean, you are a boaster and a braggart." To which Dizzy replied, "Lady, it ain't braggin' if you've done it."

Remember Dizzy's words: "It ain't braggin' if you've done it".

Joe Namath promised a victory for the Jets before the Super Bowl. Why? The thought of failure to reach his stated goal was completely mortifying, so he knew it would push him to greater heights and a greater performance. If you're afraid to publicly or privately communicate your goal to someone else, then it's not a goal. It is that simple.

Kevin Young was an Olympic hurdler. In the 1992 Olympic Games in Barcelona, he did two remarkable things. First, he won the Gold medal in the 400 meter hurdles and more amazing, he broke the oldest standing record at that time in track and field. Edwin Moses held the previous longstanding record since 1983. Edwin Moses' time was 47.02 seconds; Kevin Young's previous best prior to the Games was 47.63.

How did he do it? First, he set a goal – 47 seconds flat. Then he took 47 pieces of white paper with the number "47" written on them and taped them up all over his dorm room at the Olympic Village. His time frame was obvious – the final race. And of course, he told his coach and his teammates about his goal; in fact it was fairly obvious to anyone who saw his room.

Kevin Young went from just another medal contender – he wasn't even the favorite or the fastest – to the World record holder, and he used this systematic goal setting method.

IV. Set High and Low Goals. Another element of good goal setting is to have both high and low goals. Poet Robert Browning explained high goals perfectly: "A man's reach should exceed his grasp, or what's a heaven for?"

A low goal should be like Disraeli, the British statesman and prime minister, said: "A goal once set, then death or victory."

Now you have a goal for the number of presentations you make by number per week. It is written down. It has a time frame, the smaller the better. And you've told someone important about your goal. You also have a high goal, written down – ten presentations per week – and a low goal, written down – nine presentations per week.

In most types of sales there are two kinds of presentations: First-time presentations and follow-up presentations. With that in mind, you must continually feed your pipeline with new customers. Every company has attrition, and all industry sectors have consolidations and bankruptcies. It is critical to increase your number of first-time presentations without sacrificing follow-up visits. If you successfully increase your first-time visits per week, then your follow-up visits will naturally increase.

Trade in Your Horsepower for Purchasing Power

I was on the "bookfield" selling books door-to-door for three summers and then recruited and trained students to sell for another two summers. Here's how I implemented this goal setting system in the book business.

First, I set a goal of 180 presentations per week. That's right, 30 demonstrations a day, six days a week. I worked an average of 84 hours per week, six days a week.

I had horsepower and I was willing to trade it for purchasing power. I broke every day into three periods:

- 7:30 a.m. to noon
- Noon to 5 p.m.
- 5 p.m. to 9:30 p.m.

I set a low goal of 10 prospects per period and a high goal of 12 per period. I shared all of this with my manager, and I tracked my results every day on a 3x5 card I carried in my pocket. My time frame was 13 weeks, and if I saw 180 people a week for 13 weeks, I won the "Gold Award," the coveted award given to the salespeople who reached their goals for number of presentations.

Throughout my career, I've built several successful sales organizations in the banking industry. My salespeople at these companies set goals to see an average of 12 banks per week, with three of those twelve being new prospects. Salespeople called on banks four days a week and spent one day in the office setting appointments and making follow-up calls by phone. In each situation, my sales teams used the same goal-setting process to increase the number of presentations they made, and it worked every time if they did.

In Review

- There are three determinants of success in sales – the first is the number of prospects you see.

- The guiding principle of this determinant is: The more prospects you see, the more you sell.

- Goal setting helps you increase your number of presentations. There are four elements to good goal setting:

  1. Write it Down
  2. Set a Time Frame
  3. Tell Someone
  4. Set High and Low Goals

- Implement your goal setting system by trading in your horsepower for purchasing power.

"Professional salespeople develop strategies for even the hardest prospects, strategies to see them and to sell them."

Chapter

Xtreme Appointment Setting

The Power of the Mind

Now you have the goal of increasing your number of presentations, but how do you do it? I don't believe in hocus-pocus or magical spells, but I do believe strongly in the power of the mind. If you have done this goal setting process as I described it, then your mind will begin to figure out a way to get it done.

But your mind needs your help, so let's get into some specific actions for setting and reaching your goals. If you're making appointments to give presentations as opposed to cold calling, then you must make even more phone calls for those appointments. Here are three ideas I've taught to my sales organizations to set more phone appointments and increase your activity.

I. The Power of the Prospect List

Ah, the prospect list. I required every salesperson to have a list of 50 new prospects at all times. The list can be typed or handwritten. Each entry should include the company name, the individual contact name, and the phone number.

> *"A salesperson without a prospect list of potential new customers is soon unemployed."*

The list must be on an actual hard copy piece of paper. Why? Computers are wonderful, but I've never seen salespeople calling from their laptops a 100 percent of the time. I'm sure there are exceptions; but you need a list on a piece of paper. With a tangible list, you can call from anywhere any time you have down time: In a waiting room, on a plane, in the car, from the bathroom, you get the idea. A salesperson without a prospect list of potential new customers is soon unemployed.

In the door-to-door book business, at each doorstep we asked for the neighbors' names and wrote them all down. This was our prospect list. In the banking services business, salespeople generally had 200 community banks to call on annually, and 50 of those remained on a call list at all times.

Here are a couple of other examples of prospect lists:

New agents for Northwestern Mutual are required to have 25 new leads a week to feed into their pipeline. They are required to ask for referrals during the week while giving presentations, and each morning they are expected to call on these referrals for two-hour or three-hour blocks of time.

At one regional bank, salespeople use a software program that generates no fewer than ten new leads a day for each bank officer based on the day's transactions. This ensures that prospect lists never dry up.

Hey you! Pay attention, I'm a prospect!

Patty, an Irish American friend of mine, was coming out of his Parish church and saw his friend, Mike. "How did it go?" Mike asked Patty.

"I got excommunicated for six months," said Patty.

"That's terrible!" said Mike. "What happened?"

"It's not that bad," said Patty. "I told the priest I'd committed adultery. The priest asked me who it was. I said, 'I can't tell ya that.'

"The Priest asked, 'Was it Mrs. O'Reilly then?' I told him 'no.'"

"He said, 'Was it Mrs. O'Connor?' I said 'no.'"

"He said if I didn't tell him he was going to kick me out. I pleaded, 'Father, I can't.' He said, 'Was it Mrs. O'Shanasee?' I said 'no.'"

Then he said, 'Well alright, you're excommunicated for six months.'"

Again Mike said, "That's terrible."

"It's not that bad," said Patty. "The way I see it I got six months vacation and three good leads."

However you get them, every salesperson must have leads.

II. The Power of Time Blocking

The second idea for getting in more phone approaches, which naturally leads to more appointments and presentations, is blocking time for phone calls. Most of us have different degrees of call reluctance. Calling a new prospect is usually low on everyone's list, so people use creative avoidance to justify doing other things.

I worked with a salesperson in the banking industry who easily put in 60 hours per week. Banks aren't even open that much, but somehow he never found time for new appointments. He was a very hard working salesperson who spent all his time with the existing customer base. He just couldn't make himself call on new prospects.

To help reach the goal of making more phone calls to new prospects, you've got to block your time. The system I've found works best is this:

1. Write it on your calendar.
2. Find a quiet place and close the door (This can even be your car).

3. Be ready when it's time to call.

- Do you have your phone approach ready?
- Do you have your calendar?
- Do you have your prospect list prepared?

All of these things make your time more efficient and remove some of the psychological barriers to calling new prospects. By blocking your time, you put yourself in a place to win.

III. The Power of Controlling Your Schedule

The third idea for getting in more presentations is to schedule appointments at the best time for you and your calendar. For example, if your schedule allows you to see two prospects in the morning at 9 a.m. and 11 a.m., don't accept an appointment for 10 a.m. Most prospects will fit into your schedule, so try this next time: After a prospect has agreed to an appointment, and the prospect suggests a time that doesn't work best for you, say something like this:

"Would 9 a.m. or 11 a.m. be just as good for you as 10 a.m.?"

They'll agree almost every time. By controlling the times you set appointments, you can see more people.

Still More Excuses

One of my salespeople came up with these reasons why she didn't have more new appointments set each week:

1. Had lunch with friends (Translation: I think 12:00-to-1:00 is a bad time to call).
2. Went to the grocery store during the day (Translation: I have to eat and the store is much less crowded during work hours).
3. Played golf on Friday afternoon (Translation: No one else works on Friday afternoons).
4. Left my prospect list at home (Translation: And the dog ate it).
5. Had to get my proposals done (Translation: Couldn't miss American Idol last night. Final episode).
6. Friend had an emotional crisis (Translation: Her nail is all better now).
7. John stopped by my office for a visit (Translation: We're all caught up on the company gossip).

8. My decorator called (Translation: She doesn't work at night, so what choice did I have).
9. I had to pay my bills (Translation: Couldn't concentrate at home).
10. I wasn't feeling well (Translation: I stayed out way too late last night).
11. I have already called everyone in my territory (Translation: I think I'm all out of excuses).

> ## *"...excuses are nothing more than some very creative avoidance."*

All of these excuses are nothing more than some very creative avoidance. Salespeople use creative avoidance to make excuses not to get on the phone. If you're serious about your success and you think of yourself as a professional, track the number of new prospects you call each week and find a way to increase it by ten percent. If you do, you'll give yourself a ten percent increase in sales… and you can figure out what that means to you financially.

You're a Professional … So Act Like One

If you're really a pro, you'll write down your goal to increase new phone approaches, set a time frame to increase it, and then tell someone important you're going to do it.

For example, my salespeople in the banking business set appointments with 85 percent of the bankers they talk to on the phone. So, to get three new presentations per week, they must call five new bankers per week. To see four new banks per week they could simply increase the number of new calls to six. The number of new presentations then increases, and sales will follow the same increasing trend assuming no change in the quality of your presentation or the quality of the prospect.

If you work for a cold call sales organization and want to increase the number of new presentations you make, here are a few simple ways to accomplish this:

• Increase the amount of time you work.
• Be more efficient in your workday by spending less time with each prospect.
• Spend less time doing non-job related activities during prime work hours.

Breaking Through the Excuses

If you truly believe that you've seen all the potential customers in your area, talk to management. But the truth is not that you've seen all the good prospects. Instead, I've found that salespeople believe their own excuses to justify why they aren't seeing more people, excuses like:

- I've seen everyone.
- I was there last year.
- I've called 100 times and can't get in.
- They're loyal to a competitor.

It's not really that you've seen everyone. You have just seen all the easy ones! Professional salespeople develop strategies for even the hardest prospects, strategies to see them and to sell them.

Michelle sells printers and copiers to high-end businesses. She uses a technique that she finds highly effective when she's working in an area that seems to be all "worked over." When prospects give her the excuse that someone from her company or a competitor has already been there, she is relieved.

"Oh good!" she will say. "It's great to run into someone who is familiar with our products. I bet you didn't know we have added a new product line that has saved our clients thousands of dollars and greatly added to their efficiency. I'd love to tell you about it."

> *"It pays to be creative in selling. If it were easy, everyone would do it!"*

Remember it will always be easier to see an existing customer than a new one; it will always be harder to overcome call reluctance than visit an old friend. If this is holding you back from increasing your new presentations or your total presentations, then make your calendar help you. Say to yourself, I have "x" amount of time for old prospects and existing clients and "x" amount of time for new prospects. Mark that time on your calendar. Set a goal and then work toward it.

One common excuse you must avoid is the use of the "travel budget" crutch. Personally, I've never heard of a salesperson being fired for going over his expense budget if he or she was also the best salesperson. Management may whine, but they all want the same thing: More sales.

Jonathan Goody was the top salesperson in one of my sales organizations. Jonathan was always over his budget for travel, typically $1,000 a month more than the next highest salesperson's expenses. He would jump on an airplane at the drop of a hat; he stayed at more expensive hotels than most, and he ate better, too. No matter how much we asked him to lower his expenses, he never did.

So, we fired him. No, the truth is, we paid gladly to have all that production! No one is going to fire a top producer for going over his budget; but weak salespeople do get replaced for going over their expense budgets or falsifying their reports.

Work Smart, Not Hard

Maybe you don't make excuses and you work really hard. That's great, but the problem some salespeople have in maximizing their performance is that they often spin their wheels and never get anywhere. Unless you're in front of a prospect you can't get results. That's why the number of people you see is so critical. The question you have to ask yourself is this: Are you a peak performer or do you work harder and harder and seem to keep "spinning your wheels?"

Hamsters run hard, but they never get anywhere. Start focusing on how to maximize the benefits of every situation, and you will find yourself much less frustrated and increase your presentations just by doing a little thinking and planning.

The Multiplier Effect

Another thought about increasing activity in regard to the number of presentations you give weekly is this: The more presentations you give, the better you get at each presentation. You get a "multiplier effect". Practice makes perfect and the more you practice, the better you should get if your head is in the game.

Larry was a student who cleverly crammed four years of education into six. He sold books for six summers and was one of the top rookies in The Southwestern Company, but Larry never got any better each subsequent summer. The number of presentations he gave each week never varied much over his six years on the bookfield, and his results never did either. Larry had one year's worth of experience six separate times. More presentations don't always mean better presentations, but they should until you're at the top of your sales organization – then they should keep you there.

There are a lot of things to do to get out of a sales slump. One great way to bust through a slump is by increasing your activity to move faster through negativity. It's a simple way to fix a big problem: Just focus on increasing the number of new presentations you give until you get to buyers again. As you work to increase your presentations, you'll find that not only will you beat the slumps, but you'll get through them faster.

Maybe you are one of the salespeople who believe in "quality not quantity." You may be of the mindset that three great presentations and three great prospects are better than nine bad presentations and nine bad prospects. That's right; I agree with that.

But won't you agree that nine great presentations to nine great prospects would be the best of both worlds? That's what you should be striving for, and that's what great salespeople do day-in and day-out.

"No" is a Part of "Yes"

Morgan gave more presentations than anyone in the organization, but Rita outsold him because she sold half of the people she saw. However, it took several years until she began to realize that she needed to increase her activity with new prospects.

What did it? Two new salespeople outperformed her in activity and results. The competition finally got her. You may have had a higher closing percentage, but eventually someone's going to out-work you; and the sales profession favors the salesperson who believes in the law of averages. This year, if you are number one in sales but not number one in activity, someone's gonna claim your title sooner or later.

> *"The law of averages really is a law. And ultimately you can't break it."*

Every "no" is a part of a "yes." In fact, learn to love the "no" answers, because more activity equals more of those. As I left a house in the door-to-door book business, I'd always say: "Thank you for the "no." Every "no" is part of a "yes", and

I have to get a certain number of "no's" to get a 'yes.'"

In one particular house, I went on to say: "That's the nicest "no" I've had all day. You're my third "no" in a row, so a "yes" is right around the corner."

As I turned to leave, the woman at the house said, "Come back! I don't want to be a 'no.'"

Nothing is sweeter to a salesperson that hearing "yes", but in professional selling, our job is to get "no's" too.

In Review

- Here are some ideas to increase your number of appointments:

  1. Start a prospect list and keep it growing. A salesperson without a prospect list of potential new customers is soon unemployed.
  2. Block time for phone calls on your calendar to avoid creative avoidance.
  3. Ask yourself these questions before you begin calling in your blocked time:

     - Do you have your phone approach ready?
     - Do you have your calendar?
     - Do you have your prospect list prepared?

  4. Schedule appointments at the best time for you.

- Here are some simple ways to break through the excuses:

  1. Remember it will always be easier to see an existing customer than a new one.
  2. The more presentations you give, the better you get at each presentation, and so you get a multiplier effect.
  3. Every "no" is a part of a "yes."

*"What the mind can conceive and believe,
it can achieve."*

Chapter 4

Laying Foundations for a Great Presentation with Attitude

Let's say that you're with me so far:

- You believe in the law of averages.
- You've set a high and low goal to increase your activity.
- You've written it down.
- You've told someone important about your goal.
- You've set a time frame.
- You've answered your own excuses.
- You've committed to a plan to raise your activity with new prospects.

Now, it's time to move to the second pillar of success in the sales saga: The quality of your presentation.

Attitude is Irrelevant

Every great performer knows that *spectacular* performance is always preceded by *unspectacular* preparation. So there are some foundations that must be laid for a great presentation. The first brick in the foundation is attitude. This may come as a surprise to you, but attitude does not necessarily determine results in sales. I've known hundreds of salespeople who go out and sell successfully with bad attitudes.

Lynn's best sales year was the year she interviewed for new jobs because she didn't like the one she had. The number one salesperson in the door-to-door book business one summer – out of several thousand students – called his sales manager to quit every week because he didn't like going door-to-door.

It is possible to sell with a bad attitude. How? Success in sales is based on the number of people you see, the quality of your presentation, and the quality of your prospects. Great actors and actresses give great performances with bad attitudes and they give great performances when they are sick. On the other hand, a bad attitude can affect your results if you let it affect your effort and performance.

"What's behind the door I cannot tell, But I know the more I open, the more I sell."

Instead of harboring a bad attitude after hearing your tenth "no" of the day, or getting lost, or spilling coffee on your computer, try saying this little poem under your breath: "What's behind the door I cannot tell, But I know the more I open, the more I sell."

You never know, it just might make you smile. And what's the old saying: "Fake it 'til you make it!"

William James, a Harvard Psychologist, once said: "The mind can't tell the difference between real and artificial stimulus." If you tell yourself you feel healthy, happy, and terrific, you will feel healthy, happy, and terrific. James went on to say, "People can alter their lives by altering their attitudes."

If you have attitude problems – and most of us do at some point – here are some thoughts to help you get a professional attitude as a foundation for a high quality presentation.

I. Utilize Affirmations

Use positive affirmations. Olympic athletes use psychological conditioning and it works. They visualize themselves winning the race or breaking the record. What the mind can conceive and believe, it can achieve.

Here are some affirmations I've used and a few that other salespeople have shared with me over the years. Speak these aloud in front of the mirror or anytime you need a mental boost:

- I feel healthy, happy, and terrific.
- I can, I will, I am going to become the greatest salesperson in the history of the company.
- I am nature's greatest miracle. (From *The Greatest Salesman in the World*)
- When the going gets tough, the tough get going.
- I will go over, under, around, and through any obstacle that stands in my way.
- I am the best.

- Today opportunity knocks and I answer.
- I dare to be great; I dare to create my future now.
- Write it on your heart – today is the day, now is the time.

You think these sound hokey? You don't need these? Corny affirmations aren't cool? I don't think legendary Olympic athletes Carl Lewis, Marion Jones, Eric Heyden, or Mark Spitz were worried about getting their "cool cards" punched. They wanted to win Gold medals, and I hope you do too. Or at least the gold part.

II. Find Happiness in the Journey

Here is a great quote I want you to memorize: "Happiness is a way of traveling; not some place you arrive. Most people are about as happy as they make up their minds to be."

Unfortunately, I didn't think of it, Abe did. One of our most famous presidents, Abraham Lincoln, said that.

I've got a long leash, designer collar, the big yard, and the gourmet dog food. How come I'm not happy?

When my friend, Mike, graduated from college, he thought he would be happy. He was the first one in his family to get a degree, but he soon learned that a degree did not make him happy. So, he got a sales job and started earning an above-average income, but that didn't make him happy either. He looked around and wondered, what is making people happy? A lot of people had big houses, so he got one. That didn't make him happy. What could it be? He saw his friends getting wives, so he got one of those too. Guess what? That didn't make him happy either.

What Mike finally realized is that it isn't achievement, money, possessions, or someone else that could make him happy. He learned that happiness truly is, as Abe said, a way of traveling and not some place you arrive.

There are people without an education who are working for minimum wage, renting an apartment, and driving an old used car who will go to bed tonight happy. Yet here in the richest country in the world, other people will lay their heads down in million dollar homes with all the riches in the world and they are unhappy. Your attitude and happiness is yours to control.

There is a thought among people that happiness is something they only find outside their careers. But there is nothing more fulfilling than a lifetime of success in your profession. Stop looking everywhere else; happiness is already in the car with you.

Happiness is a Journey, not a Destination...

> *"For a long time it seemed to me that life was about to begin – real life. But there was always some obstacle in the way, something to be gotten through first, some unfinished business, time still to be served, a debt to be paid. At last it dawned on me that these obstacles were my life. This perspective has helped me to see there is no way to happiness. Happiness is the way. So treasure every moment you have and remember that time waits for no one."*

– John Phillip Souza

III. Read Inspirational Material

You can significantly affect your attitude thorough reading inspirational material. Here are some books I find truly inspiring that help me get my attitude right. Of course, you can find your own, but these are a good place to start:

- *The Bible*
- *The Greatest Salesman in the World*
- *Tuesdays with Morey*

- *Who Moved my Cheese*
- *How I Raised Myself from Failure to Success in Selling*
- *Winners Never Quit*
- *Chicken Soup for the Soul*
- *The Seven Habits of Highly Effective People*
- *Think and Grow Rich!*
- *48 Days to the Work You Love*
- *How to Win Friends and Influence People*
- *The Purpose Driven Life*
- *How to Stop Worrying and Start Living*
- *The Prophet*

Inspirational material can help douse our selfish natures with positive messages that take our minds off ourselves and onto our purpose. It also helps us realize that most obstacles are beatable.

After all, who wouldn't be inspired by stories like these? Remember Kerri Strug's chilling performance in the 1996 Olympics? Believing the team gold medal was on the line, Strug took to the second vault on a badly sprained left ankle and stuck the landing for a score of 9.712. In the same 1996 Olympics in track and field, a week after dropping out of the heptathlon with a severely strained right hamstring, Jackie Joyner-Kersee leaped from fifth to third and the bronze medal in her final attempt of the long jump.

How about the attitude and grit of one player in Game One of the 1988 World Series? With a strained left hamstring and sprained right knee, pinch hitter Kirk Gibson hit a full-count, two-out homer in the bottom of the ninth to give the Dodgers a 5-4 win over the Athletics. L.A. won the series 4-1, essentially on the momentum of that homerun.

All of these extraordinary people could have thrown in the towel and no one would have blamed them. But they didn't. Their attitude to never give up, to win, is what made the difference. The point here is not that you should keep selling when you are suffering from a pulled hammy. I only want you to keep a good attitude so that it doesn't affect your performance, and instead your attitude inspires you to give greater performances.

IV. Make Lemonade

Another element of your attitude is your disposition toward obstacles. Sam Johnson, a legendary sales manager for the Southwestern Company, used to say, "In every seeming adversity, there is a seed for greater growth."

We've all heard of making lemonade from lemons. Here are some examples:

Lemon: *My territory got changed or reduced.*
Lemonade: *Now I have less drive time and can focus my efforts.*

Lemon: *The competition lowered their price below ours.*
Lemonade: *They obviously can't compete on the merits of the product.*

Lemon: *I just lost a major account.*
Lemonade: *I have more time to develop a new and larger account.*

Lemon: *Some of my customers have been receiving the wrong shipments.*
Lemonade: *I can find a more efficient process to eliminate error.*

Lemon: *I just got a new sales manager and we don't seem to get along.*
Lemonade: *Now I have a chance to practice my personality style-flexing.*

Lemon: *Our product line has been cut down.*
Lemonade: *I can hone my presentations of our best products.*

Lemon: *The GPS in my car is not working.*
Lemonade: *This will give me a chance to learn the area a little better.*

"Is your proverbial glass of water half full or half empty?"

Here is a good example of how attitude can make the difference. A very large national shoe manufacturer decided to expand their territory into some African countries, and they decided to send their very best salesperson to do the job.

A few months later having totally failed to sell any shoes, he called the company and said: "I'm returning on the next flight. I can't sell shoes here. Everybody goes barefoot!"

Discouraged and ready to give up on their expansion plans, they sent in a rookie. He broke every sales record in the company's history. They asked him how he was able to achieve this kind of success when their star salesman had utterly failed.

The rookie responded: "The prospects are unlimited. Nobody wears shoes here!"

You see, the difference in the two men was a simple matter of perspective and attitude. Is your proverbial glass of water half full or half empty?

Remember the Pony

There once were two 10-year-old twin brothers. One was an optimist, and the other a pessimist. They were twins, but they seemed so different. This frustrated their parents, so they took the boys to a psychiatrist to be tested. The psychiatrist said he had a test for such boys.

He put the pessimist in a room full of toys and then put the optimist in a room full of horse manure.

The psychiatrist waited a few minutes and went back to see the pessimistic boy. Sure enough, he was sitting in the middle of the room crying.

"Why didn't you play with the ball?" the psychiatrist asked the boy.

"I was afraid it would hit me in the chin," the lad replied.

"Why didn't you play with the balloons?" asked the psychiatrist.

"I was afraid they'd pop and scare me," replied the boy.

"Why didn't you pop the gun?" the doctor asked.

"I was afraid it would shoot me," said the pessimist.

The psychiatrist shook his head and went to the room with the optimist. When he opened the door, the boy was in the middle of the room throwing horse manure everywhere.

"Stop! Stop! What are you doing?" yelled the psychiatrist.

The little boy turned, covered head-to-toe in horse manure. "Mister," he said. "With all this horse manure in here, I know somewhere there has to be a pony!"

The right attitude allows you to be happy and helps you to not get discouraged in the face of obstacles. It also allows you to be persistent. When you get discouraged, just remember: That pony is in there somewhere.

In Review

- Attitude doesn't determine results.

- Success in sales is based on the number of people you see, the quality of your presentation, and the quality of your prospects.

- The mind can't tell the difference between real and artificial stimulus.

- Here are four elements to improve your attitude as a foundation for a high quality presentation:

    1. Utilize Affirmations: Look in the Mirror and tell yourself you feel happy, healthy, and terrific.

  2. Find Happiness in the Journey: Be happy just to be on the road of life, not at some mythical destination.
  3. Read Inspirational Material: Find inspiration in the struggles and triumphs of others.
  4. Make Lemonade: Develop a positive disposition toward obstacles.

Chapter 5

More Attitude Bricks for the Foundation

Persistence is All-Powerful

Arguably the greatest President in our nation's history, a recounting of Abraham Lincoln's career leading up to his election illustrates is a tale of the utmost persistence. His failures far exceeded his successes. Just look at this timeline of Abe's life:

1832 – Lost his job
1832 – Defeated in the race for the legislature
1833 – Failed in business
1834 – Elected to legislature
1835 – Sweetheart died
1836 – Suffered a nervous breakdown
1838 – Defeated for speaker in the legislature
1843 – Defeated for nomination for Congress
1846 – Elected to Congress
1848 – Lost re-nomination to Congress
1849 – Rejected for job as land officer
1854 – Defeated for Senate
1856 – Defeated for nomination for Vice-President
1858 – Defeated for Senate
1860 – Elected 16th president of the United States

It's a truly inspiring story, with almost 30 years of handling crushing disappointment. But Lincoln never quit, and in the end, his unfailing persistence reshaped an entire country.

In the midst of the worst depression in our country's history, Calvin Coolidge had these words to say: "Nothing in the world can take the place of persistence. Talent will not; nothing is more common than unsuccessful men with talent. Genius will not; unrewarded genius is almost a proverb. Education will not; the world is full of educated derelicts. Persistence and determination alone are omnipotent. The slogan 'Press On' has solved and always will solve the problems of the human race."

"Persistence truly is all-powerful."

A Tale of Sheer Persistence

Eddie Shore was a legendary hockey player, a defenseman for the Boston Bruins. Eddie missed his team's train to play for the Stanley Cup in Montreal on January 2, 1929. Eddie believed that nothing could be more catastrophic or embarrassing than missing a game.

There just didn't seem to be a way to get to that game. It was 9 p.m., and there were no trains to Montreal until too late the next day. There was no chance for a flight because of a freezing rain that engulfed the area. After several calls, Eddie contacted a friend who offered him his limousine and chauffeur for the journey to Montreal.

By that point, a sleet storm was tearing Boston apart, but Eddie was unfazed. The chauffeur came for him at 11:30 p.m., and they began the 350-mile Boston-to-Montreal drive over dilapidated roads that wound around the New England mountains, which were completely covered with sheets of ice and snow.

Shore asked the driver to hurry. "The man apologized," Shore said, "and told me he didn't have chains, and furthermore didn't like driving in the winter. The poor fellow urged me to turn back to Boston."

Shore was not about to give up that easily. He bought chains and decided to do the driving himself into the blizzard as it approached with full force. Snow caked on either side of the lone windshield wiper, which eventually froze to the glass. "I couldn't see out of the window," Shore recalled, "so I had to remove the top half of the windshield."

Shore steered the limousine across the Massachusetts border and up into the New Hampshire mountains, dangerously exposed to the icy wind.

"At about five in the morning," Shore said, "we began losing traction. The tire chains had worn out."

Luckily, he found a road construction camp nearby. Shore awakened the watchman and got a new set of tire chains, then continued toward Canada. The road was icier than a hockey rink, and the car skidded off the road four times, but each time Shore and his terrified chauffeur managed to push it back on the highway.

Exhausted and frozen, Shore finally asked the chauffeur to drive while he took a quick nap. Shore quickly fell asleep, but minutes later, the chauffeur lost control and the car dove into a ditch. Unwilling to give up this battle, Shore hiked a mile to a farmhouse.

"I paid eight dollars for a team of horses," Shore recalls. "I harnessed them and pulled the car out of the ditch. By this time, we weren't far from Montreal, and I thought we'd still make it before game time."

They did . . . and the sight of his "abominably snow-covered defenseman" awed Art Ross, the Bruins coach.

"His eyes were bloodshot," Ross said, "his face frostbitten and wind burned, his fingers bent and set like claws after gripping the wheel so long. He couldn't even walk straight."

Ross insisted that Shore not dress for the game that night against Montreal, but Eddie refused to sit this one out. He took the ice for Boston and played 56 minutes of the 60-minute game. He missed four minutes because he had a pair of two-minute penalties.

Was the trip worth it? Well, Boston won the Stanley Cup match, 1-0, and Eddie scored the game's only goal. It was an extraordinarily courageous performance.

"Persistence through failure is what will cause you to be successful."

Setbacks Don't Have to = Failure

As both a salesperson and a member of society, many times you are going to find circumstances will be different than what you want them to be. Many times you will find circumstances discouraging. Many times in the process of trying to reach your goals you will fail. Persistence through failure is what will cause you to be successful. Eddie Shore was given impossible circumstances and immense discouragement, and he failed many times in trying to reach his destination. But persistence through failure and impossible circumstances enabled him to reach his goal.

Eddie Shore was the embodiment of the Air Force slogan: "The difficult we do immediately; the impossible takes a little longer."

When I look up the word *persistence* in the dictionary, I want to see your picture. As you focus on increasing your activity – more new presentations – and work on improving the quality of your presentation, a persistent attitude will be one of your most valuable tools.

The Best Can Get Better

Another part of your attitude should be a burning desire to improve your performance and your results. If your attitude is one of "what I'm doing is good enough", then obviously you won't improve. But remember this: Sales is a down escalator, and if you stand still, you will go backwards. When you're green, you grow; when you're ripe, you rot.

Charlie "Tremendous" Jones, the famed inspirational author and speaker, used to say: "You're the same person ten years from now except for two things: The people you meet and the books you read." (Let's add CDs and DVDs to that to modernize the quote.)

So, part of your attitude should be your commitment to improve as a professional. There is no other notable profession that doesn't require continuing education: Doctors, lawyers, airplane pilots, and countless others. Be great! Require it of yourself! Listen to CD's, go to seminars, and read books. You cannot be too busy chopping wood to sharpen the axe.

Think Big

Another part of a great attitude is the ability to think big. Countless salespeople have pushed through slumps, found inspiration, or were able to persist because they believed in the home run. They thought big, like the kid in the following story.

One day a salesman left his house for work and passed the neighborhood kid on the way to the bus stop. The young boy had put up a sign that read,

"Puppy, 50 cents."

Sure enough, there beside the sign sat a dirty little puppy. The salesman knew the boy wasn't thinking big enough, so he told the young boy to wash the puppy, brush his coat, put a big bow on him, and raise the price.

And as the salesman got on the bus to go to work, he told the boy, "Remember, just think big."

That evening as he passed the boy's house, there was a new sign that said, "Puppy $10,000", and across the sign was boldly written, "SOLD". The salesman thought this was worth being late for supper to investigate, so he went and knocked on the boy's door.

When the boy came to the door, the salesman asked, "Son, how much did you get for that puppy?"

The boy stated, "Ten thousand dollars."

"How exactly did you arrive at that price?" asked the salesman with wonder.

"Well," said the boy, "you said to think big, and 10,000 is the biggest number I could think of!"

Still perplexed, the salesman asked, "OK, how much did you really get for that dog?"

"I got $10, 000," said the boy again.

The bewildered salesman persisted and asked again about the sale price. The young boy told him with pride, "Yep that's right, ten thousand bucks. I took two $5000 cats in trade."

"Remember, just think big..."

Just like the boy at the beginning of the story, we all limit ourselves by what we think.

But as the great salesman Og Mandino says: "We are nature's greatest miracle."

You can increase your value a hundred-fold if you just believe it.

Well, I'd say that sale went pretty well. I guess it pays to think BIG.

Developing a Service Attitude

Have you ever been shopping for something, and you could literally see the dollar signs in the salesperson's eyes? (Believe me, your prospects can see the dollar signs in your eyes if your attitude is one of do anything to make the sale.) That is why a service attitude should also be an inherent part of your attitude.

William Penn, historic figure and founder of Pennsylvania, said: "I expect to pass through life but once. If therefore there be any kindness I can show, or any good thing I can do to any fellow human being, let me do it now as I shall not pass this way again."

If you always give to get, you'll never get. But if you give to give, you'll get. Whatever you put into the lives of others will come back into your own. It's pretty simple, really. Put out good – you'll get good. Put out bad – you'll get bad.

Steve sold check sorters to banks. One day, one of the banks he called on didn't need any sorters, but the banker was upset because their printer had just broken. He asked Steve what he thought about the various printer brands and where he might shop for them.

Steve made his living by selling sorters, not printers, and he could have easily have said he didn't know or could have given him a short and easy answer. Instead, Steve did the banker's homework for him. He gave the banker names, phone numbers, and prices so the banker could check and compare printers for himself.

When it came time two years later for that banker to buy a sorter, that banker called only one person – Steve. Steve was the kind of salesperson that banker wanted to do business with. Your prospects want to work with a salesperson with a service minded attitude.

"...there's another deposit in the sales bank for withdrawal later."

I think back over the thousands of times someone asked me to do something that I didn't make a dime on, and always I strived to do whatever was asked of me. When I went out of my way to help a prospect or a customer, I said to myself, "Well, there's another deposit in the sales bank for withdrawal later."

To top it off, I did it all cheerfully. Nothing sells like a service attitude, and believe me, the prospect can tell.

P.T. Barnum said: "You can fool some of the people all the time, and all of the people sometimes, but you can never fool all of the people all the time."

And I say, "Why try?" It's so much easier to have a service attitude all the time as you pass through life.

Ryan had just that sort of service attitude. One summer on the bookfield, he was giving a terrific presentation. Suddenly in the middle of his close, the woman got a phone call and was thrown into a state of panic. She had to leave immediately, but could not take her children with her; she couldn't leave them alone either.

Without even thinking, Ryan volunteered to watch the kids until she could return.

The woman agreed and rushed out the door. Hours later she returned, so thankful for Ryan's thoughtful offer to help. And guess what? He even got a sale out of it. And the woman's family and friends bought from him all summer long.

When he went to other houses in the neighborhood, the homeowners would ask him: "Are you that boy who helped watch Sheila's kids?"

Then they bought books, too. Going above and beyond what is expected will never hurt you; it will only help.

I. Leave Your Comfort Zone

To be great in selling, you must have a willingness to leave your comfort zone. I've never met a great salesperson who did not leave his comfort zone.

Sometimes it's in the approach. You just hate to make a cold call, knock on a door, or pick up the phone and call someone you don't know.

Sometimes it's in the set-up. You just hate to ask the prospects questions about their business, their children, or whatever.

Sometimes it's when you close. You just hate to bring the prospect to a point of decision.

Sometimes it's in the follow-up. You just hate to hear another objection or stall.

Sometimes it's when you ask for money or payment. You say: "Can't we just send them a bill?"

Maybe it's all of these, but whatever it is that's uncomfortable, to be great you must overcome it.

For me, it's the close. When I was selling books for the Southwestern Company, laundry day would come, and I'd be surprised each week at how fast the toes of my socks were wearing out. I thought it was the brand of socks I was buying, and then it dawned on me – I dug my toes into my shoes every time I closed.

That's how I dealt with the uncomfortable feeling of asking a prospect to buy. Get your own trick that gets you through it, but get through it and stop making excuses.

Great pro baseball players swing a bat the way a coach taught them, not like they would naturally. They left their comfort zones. Part of your attitude must be that you are willing to be emotionally uncomfortable in order to perform at the highest level.

Say what you want... my mind may be warm, but my body's COLD!

II. Know that Selling is a Profession

A critical and often overlooked element of your attitude is to always remember that you are a professional. After all, sales is a profession. What do most people think of when you say the word "salesperson?" A few words come to mind:

- Pushy
- High pressure
- Conman
- Charlatan
- Cheat
- Dishonest
- Crooked
- Twist your arm
- Make you buy
- Say anything to get the sale

It's true that even some salespeople would describe sales using these words. That is because some salespeople are all of those things!

Salespeople in general have a bad image, frankly, because there have been so many bad ones. A professional attitude will set you apart. You can change the image of the pushy, plaid-suited, greasy salesperson. Make up your mind that you're going to be proud you're in sales, and then act like it. It is impossible – yes, impossible – to give a great presentation when you don't believe you are a great professional salesperson.

Robert Louis Stevenson said we all sell something – a product, an idea, or a service. The best attorney is the best communicator, not the one who knows the most law. The best preacher or priest is the best communicator, not the one who knows the most about the *Bible*. The best teacher is the best communicator, not the one who knows the most about the material she is teaching.

> ## *"At the primary level, sales is just effective communication."*

Some of the most successful people in every profession got their start in sales:

- Harry Truman, U.S. President – Sold Men's Clothing
- Billy Graham, Evangelist – Sold Fuller Brushes
- Carli Fiorina, Former CEO Hewlett Packard – Ma Bell Salesperson
- Ken Starr, Prominent attorney – Sold books door-to-door in college
- Rick Perry, Governor of Texas – Sold books door-to-door in college
- Mark Heard, CEO of Hewlett Packard – NCR Salesperson
- Bruce Henderson, Founder of the Boston Group – Sold books door-to-door in college
- Greg Daily, CEO of iPayment – Sold Christmas trees

Those are some of the most successful leaders of our time, and that's just a short list of the greats who got their start in sales – be proud you're in that fraternity.

III. Don't Be Afraid of Change

Finally, part of your attitude should be a willingness to accept change. All great salespeople must be willing to accept change. *Who Moved My Cheese* is an excellent book that explains this principal. In the book, Spencer Johnson discusses the three stages of change: Preparing for change, gaining "change skills", and achieving a change.

I recommend the book; it's a fast read.

Charles Darwin said in his classic, *Origin of Species*: "It is not the strongest of the species that survives, nor the most intelligent, but the ones who are most responsive to change."

Throughout my career, I've witnessed many salespeople fail because somebody "moved their cheese" and they refused to change. The only thing constant in a vibrant, free market economy is change. As a salesperson, you should embrace change, love change, and realize that it is change that gives you new opportunities. Without change in the marketplace, there is no new opportunity. If a caterpillar becomes a butterfly and an ugly duckling becomes a swan, then think of what change can do for you.

In Review

• Review the attitude checklist for the foundations of giving a great presentation:

  1. I used positive affirmations.
  2. I read inspirational material frequently.
  3. I believe I am as happy as I want to be.
  4. I believe I can go over, under, around, or through any obstacle to get the job done.
  5. I believe persistence alone is omnipotent.
  6. I am committed to improvement in my performance and knowledge.
  7. I think big.
  8. I am committed to a service attitude.
  9. I am willing to leave my comfort zone.
  10. I am a professional and will act like one.
  11. I accept change willingly as a part of sales and life.

• Now you have gone a long way to laying the foundation for a great presentation. Attitude is one block upon which great presentations and great performances are built.

• A great attitude will help you give more presentations, too!

"What comes out of your mouth determines your success or failure."

Chapter

The Planned Presentation: The Only One Worth Giving

A planned presentation is not only a building block for a great performance. It is central to the entire sales process. And yet, no principle I've taught over the years has been met with more resistance. However, there is no principle I believe in any more strongly than this.

I can just hear the groans now. *"But Tom..."*

- "I don't want to sound canned."
- "I want to be flexible."
- "Every situation is different."
- "I talk to different levels of decision makers, so I need different presentations."

I say: OK, fine. Making these excuses is a lot easier than doing the work of a professional, which is planning your sales presentation.

Yes, There is a Best Presentation

I believe in a planned presentation and here is why. First, the best tool you have is your words. What comes out of your mouth determines your success or failure. If this weren't true, everyone could just send out brochures and fancy PowerPoint presentations and make six figures a year. If you believe you have value as a salesperson, then it is in the words you say when you talk to prospects. That must be a given!

There are some things you say that communicate our message better than others and lead to the results you want. Let's call these words, "the best sales presentation possible."

The best sales presentation possible is not vastly different each time. There are certain benefits and features of every product that must be communicated, and those benefits and features must be communicated in the best way possible. Best, by definition, means one, exclusive, alone; the best way is better than any other way by its very definition. There are not five best ways. There can be only one best way.

We are looking to expand our torture department. Are you familiar with PowerPoint?

Your goal is to give the best presentation you can to each and every prospect. How do you get there? You have a choice based on your experience – shoot from the hip, go with the flow, or plan your presentation. It's your choice, but the only way to give the ever-elusive "best" presentation and to give it every time is to plan it.

Here are some thoughts about why it pays to plan your presentation:

I. Have Planned Responses

If your presentation is planned, you'll have time to think about your prospects' verbal and non-verbal reactions and comments. If you have to think of what you're going to say next, you simply can't do that.

I. Gain Heightened Efficiency

Efficiency is the second advantage of planning your presentation. No non-relevant material can creep into your presentation to distract you or your prospect. You don't repeat yourself. You cover all the salient points in the most efficient manner possible.

II. Guarantee Thoroughness

Third, you guarantee that you are more thorough. Perhaps that is really just a part of efficiency, but it helps to think of it separately. You never leave anything out, and you never present important points in the wrong place in your presentation if you've planned and practiced.

"If you are only listening to yourself, you
can't listen to the prospect!"

Unplanned presentations can go on forever, leave important points out, and in general be wastes of qualified prospects' time. You can also miss important buying signs, interest signs, and signs of concern because you have to worry about what you are going to say next rather than pay attention to the nonverbal communication that is taking place. If you are only listening to yourself, you can't listen to the prospect!

III. Practice to Make Perfect

Another reason for giving a planned presentation is to better gauge your results. No professional athlete experiments with his shot, stroke, or swing. Can you imagine Pete Sampras saying to himself at Wimbledon: "You know, I think I'll try a couple of different serve motions today."

Or Kobe Bryant saying: "I'm going to shoot my jump shot differently every time this game."

Albert Pujols, baseball great with the St. Louis Cardinals, prides himself on taking the same swing every time. All the pros tweak and constantly strive to improve, but their basic motions stay the same. It's when they stray from that basic motion that they have slumps or bad games.

The same is true in sales. Great salespeople can have bad days, bad weeks, or longer slumps when they stray from their basic planned presentation.

So You Don't Want to "Sound Canned"

Maybe you are worried about sounding scripted and I know exactly what you mean. I hate telemarketers that call me with canned scripts and then just read word-for-word. We all do!

However, I love a great play or movie where the actors know the lines so well that the audience believes the actors are the characters. Well-rehearsed lines don't sound canned, but to get to that point you must practice aloud, or you can start rough and use your prospects as your dress rehearsals. The second idea isn't the most ideal, but it's better than a career of ad-libs and improv.

> ## "A planned presentation doesn't have to sound canned – you determine that."

The Zen of Flexibility

Perhaps you're thinking to yourself that you need flexibility, something a planned presentation just can't provide. What is more flexible than a mechanic with a tool-box who knows every tool intimately? The better planned your presentation, the more flexible you can be to leave a part or two out in order to tailor a benefit or feature to the specific needs of a prospect. The Zen of flexibility starts with a structure.

Maybe you are the kind of salesperson who prefers to "go with the flow". Hear this, and hear me well: Someone in the presentation is going to be in control – you or the prospect.

Spencer Hayes, business legend with a net worth of several hundred million dollars, still puts the title "salesperson" on his business card to this day. Spencer says: "In every conversation someone makes a sale and someone gets sold."

I am not saying that someone wins and someone loses. Real selling can only be win-win. I do mean, however, than someone – and let's hope it's the salesperson – is in control of the flow and direction of the conversation.

A Little Pre-Planning Goes a Long Way

One great way to control the presentation is by knowing where you are going in the presentation by pre-planning it. It is very difficult to control where you're headed unless you know where you're going. A planned presentation – if you stay with it – allows you to be in control.

A planned presentation leads the prospect in the direction you want it to go. An unplanned, free-lance, shoot-from-the-hip presentation doesn't necessarily go in the direction you want.

You may be saying to yourself: "I can go where I want and direct the process with an unplanned sales talk."

You're really saying that you can control the process. Then we agree that control is a good thing, but the question remains on the best way to do that. The answer is obvious: If there is some best, ideal presentation that we could give for our product, it can be planned.

The minute you begin to visualize the ideal perfect presentation, you have begun creating your planned presentation. So go ahead and finish the job – plan your presentation – and gain control of what's happening during your presentation.

Unplanned presentations simply make your job harder. However, if you stick to a plan that is well rehearsed, you can be more in tune with your prospect's verbal and non-verbal signals while you're talking. If you have to think of what to say next, it's very difficult to be as in tune with what else is going on around you. You can always be in tune and stay aware if you know what you're going to say next.

In Review

- There is such a thing as a "Best Presentation." It is a planned and practiced one.

- Planning your presentation pays off for many reasons: You have time to plan out your responses. You gain heightened efficiency where no non-relevant material can creep into your presentation. You guarantee thoroughness. You never leave anything important out and ensure that you don't drone on until the prospect loses interest. You can practice to always keep improving.

- Planning does not make you sound canned. In actuality, you plan so that you don't sound canned.

- With a planned presentation, you are flexible and natural in your delivery.

*"Your goal should be to get to the buying line
as quickly as possible, then close the sale."*

Chapter

And Now Introducing: "The Buying Line"

I want to introduce you to a concept I developed selling books door-to-door, an idea I've found applies to every kind of selling. It's called the "buying line". Here's what it looks like:

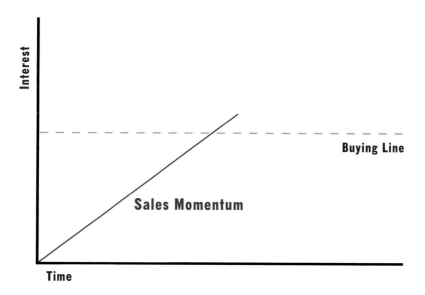

This is the principal behind the buying line: After a certain amount of time during a sales presentation or several presentations, the prospect's interest rises to the level necessary to make a favorable buying decision. Or, the interest level does not rise to the level necessary to make a favorable buying decision.

In either case, the mythical line you are trying to reach as a salesperson is the "buying line".

It seems logical that the shortest distance between two lines is the best. When you meet a prospect for the first time, you start two clocks: The time clock – how long you're with the prospect – and the interest clock – what the prospect's level of interest is in your product.

In an ideal sales situation, as time goes by the prospect's interest level rises and eventually reaches the level where the prospect is ready to buy. Of course, different prospects take different amounts of time to get to the buying line.

It's a Race, not a Nature Hike

Your goal should be to get to the buying line as quickly as possible, then close the sale. The best way to achieve this is by pre-planning your presentation. Shooting from the hip, ad-libbing, or using a completely different framework for your presentation each time is counterproductive to this goal.

Every word you say in the presence of your prospect can and will be used against you. Therefore, every word that comes out of your mouth should help you get to the buying line as soon as possible. Anything you say that distracts from building customer interest or actually causes the customer to lose interest should be eliminated from your presentation. Giving a planned presentation can best accomplish this for you.

Gaining Momentum

Bob loved to tell his prospects jokes. He thought it loosened them up, made them laugh, and showed them what a great guy he was. He also loved to throw these jokes into his presentation at different times as the mood struck him. His buying lines looked like this:

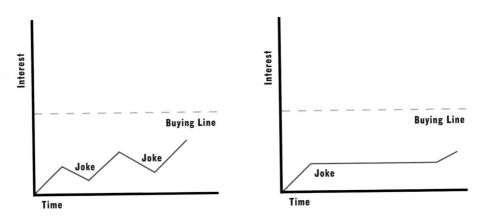

If he could have charted the effectiveness of his presentation in building customer interest to the buying line, he would have realized he was shooting himself in the foot. Sales presentations rely heavily on momentum, and anything that slows that momentum or distracts from that momentum is counter productive. Get momentum working for you, or it will end up working against you.

So a guy walks into a bar...

I sound like a broken record – or CD – but the best protection against self-fired torpedos is a planned sales talk. You can't accurately judge your performance if you give a fundamentally different presentation to each prospect.

"Make it your goal to head for the buying line
in the most direct method possible."

In Review

- Why should you plan? Let's go over the reasons you should plan your sales talk one more time:

  1. To reach the buying line in the quickest and most efficient way possible. Remember, it's a race, not a nature hike.
  2. To present your product in the most favorable light possible.
  3. To give a thorough complete accurate presentation of your product.
  4. To best control the presentation of your product.
  5. To best maintain the momentum of your presentation.
  6. To best eliminate self-fired torpedoes.
  7. To best use your and your prospect's time.

Chapter

Planned So You Don't Sound "Canned"

A Different Look at "Planned"

An insurance salesman showed up at the sales manager of a large drug company's door without an appointment. He asked to see Mr. Johnson, the sales manager, but Mr. Johnson's assistant refused, saying that her boss never sees salespeople without an appointment.

The salesman, Ed, thanked her.

"So that I might know where I'm going when I do have an appointment," he asked, "where is Mr. Johnson's office?"

"It's the second office on the third floor," the assistant said, "but you need an appointment."

Ed thanked her and promptly snuck up to the third floor. There he placed himself in Mr. Johnson's door way and waited to be noticed. Mr. Johnson finally noticed him.

"May I help you?" he asked.

"Yes," said Ed. "I am selling insurance. You wouldn't want any, would you?"

"No!" shot back Mr. Johnson.

"I didn't think so," said Ed. "If you did want some insurance, I guess you wouldn't want it from me, would you?"

Mr. Johnson was clearly irritated. "Absolutely not," he said. "You're the worst salesman I've ever seen."

"I thought you'd feel that way," Ed smiled and he turned slowly to go.

"Wait a minute," said Mr. Johnson. "Come back here. I'll buy a small policy from you if you'll let me give you a sales lesson."

Ed humbly agreed, wrote up the policy, got a check, and sat down to listen to Mr. Johnson.

"OK, first you've got to get a sales talk, " started Mr. Johnson.

"I got lots of sales talks," said Ed, "I got a whole drawer full of sales talks at my office."

"Then why didn't you use one when you came here?" Johnson asked

"I did," Ed smiled again. "That's the one I always use on sales managers."

Ed used every principal discussed so far – clarity, brevity, momentum, and planning. Selling isn't simple – you don't make the big sales by being unprepared. They don't give Academy Awards to actors or actresses who don't know their lines.

> *"...you don't make the BIG sales by being unprepared."*

Longfellow said, "The heights by great men reached and kept were not obtained by suddent flight but they while their companions slept were toiling upward in the night."

Getting to the Specifics of Planning

What goes into planning a sales presentation? Here are six recommendations:

I. Make it Word for Word. First, write it out word-for-word. Lay it aside and then reread it. Take out the superflous material, clarify the vageries, then lay it aside again. Come back to it one more time and then stop.

II. Use Constructive Critique. Second, give it to your sales manager or another very successful salesperson in your organization. Let them read it and critique it, and then make changes.

Mr. Stevens doesn't see anyone without an appointment.

III. Listen to Yourself. Next, record it. Listen to it with the script in front of you and edit it. Then listen to it again, only this time without the script in front of you – just have a pad and pen to make notes. Incorporate your notes into your final sales script. Now learn the script.

IV. Watch Yourself. Practice your script out loud in front of a mirror. Here's where we separate the women from the girls and the men from the boys because frankly, most of you won't go that far. But you should!

Fred was failing at his job selling software to banks. I went to see him to put him on probation. I felt like it was hopeless, but I wanted to give him one last chance. I worked with him all day and watched three of his presentations; they were awful.

That evening between the end of the day and dinner I had Fred give me his presentation over and over, and we worked up until midnight. I realized that night that Fred had been working for us for four months and had never really learned his presentation. The next year, Fred was our number one salesperson. He's now a sales manager for another banking services company. You know what he makes every salesperson that works for him do? That's right, learn their presentations.

Jim worked with me for 13 years. He made it to the President's Club every year, an honor bestowed upon the top producers for the year. Every time I got in the car to ride with him, he said, "I want you to listen to my sales talk."

Jim was already successful; he knew what he was doing. But he realized that even with a planned presentation things can creep into it or be left out if he wasn't dilligent. Jim was a sales professional who "drank the Kool Aid" and was successful.

V. Keep it Simple. Once you get your presentation where you want it, you must be dilligent in your efforts to keep it pure – no new unnecessary material and no exclusion of significant details. In fact, when my salespeople hit slumps, after I've looked at the number of presentations they are giving weekly and determine whether that number has dropped, this is the second place I look: Have they strayed from their presentation?

If you work for a company that has a planned script already, good! Learn it in the same way. Practice it out loud, practice it with your spouse, a good friend (only the good friends understand), your relatives, or by yourself. The point is to practice it. Ask yourself: "Am I saying anything that can be used against me?"

Think about when the President gives a speech. Someone writes it down word-for-word. The transcript is then handed out to the Press and then the President reads the speech. Why does it happen this way? One reason is so that he doesn't say something wrong that can be used against him. He always has this script to verify exactly what he said. As salespeople, we should be just as conscious of what we say to prospects.

Words can be misinterpreted and cause a serious, even a fatal disconnect between you and your propsects. Let's say you proudly state to a new prospect, "We've developed a brand new technology."

As the salesperson, you are naturally excited because it's a new feature of your product, but the prospect may say to themselves, "New is dangerous and unproven."

> *"Success in sales doesn't come from playing the good hands well..."*

It's great to believe in what you sell, but you must acknowledge and prepare for the fact that most prospects approach any sales situation with some skepticism. Sometimes a lot of skepticism. Remember that success in sales doesn't come from playing the good hands well. That's easy. It comes from playing the bad hands well!

VI. Develop an "Award Winning" Mentality Toward Planning. By now I hope you have, or least have become determined to have, a sales presentation that could win you an Oscar. A presentation that would make the famous orator Cicero proud. A better planned presentation than Aristotle could have written himself. Williams Jennings Bryant was one of the greatest American orators of all time; aspire to be better than he was. Think big.

"Think BIG."

In Review

• Remember these critical elements of planning a presentation:

1. Word for word
2. Get feedback
3. Listen to yourself
4. Watch yourself
5. KISS (Keep It Simple Salesperson)
6. Aim for an Oscar winning performance

"Goals are the initial push of the proverbial snowball down a hill that inevitably becomes an avalanche."

Chapter 9

The Art of Goal Setting

No One Succeeds Without Goals

I've covered the first two foundations for a great presentation – a great attitude and a planned, practiced, and inspired presentation to give to prospects. The third foundation of a great presentation is goal setting and tracking. I briefly discussed goal setting as it relates to the number of people you see. Now I want to give it a full discussion to show its importance throughout the entire sales process – from planning to execution and follow-up.

You need goals in at least two areas – activity and results. You should have both a high and a low goal. Your goals must be written down, have a specific timeframe, and then be communicated to someone who is important to you. Let's go through this step-by-step.

Activity Goals

First, you need activity goals. Let's say you want to track your activity in the area of approaches. A lot of salespeople use the phone for the first approach, but if you cold-call or use email, it doesn't matter. You should still set a goal for this activity. Most salespeople should set activity goals in three areas of the approach:

- Basic approaches by phone
- Email approaches
- In-person approaches

The second activity salespeople engage in is initial presentations or visits. Setting an activity goal here is both appropriate and crucial. Finally, most salespeople engage in follow-up visits or additional calls after the first meeting. It's important to set goals here as well.

Results Goals

The second types of goals are results goals. Walt and Steve were two great salespeople in one of my sales organizations, and here is how they set their goals while selling products to banks. Walt and Steve both wanted to make $100,000 a year in commissions. This was their ultimate goal. For goal setting purposes, they both set their low goal at $100,000 and their high goal at $120,000.

Walt knew that every time he sold to a bank, he earned an average of $4,000. Some sales had higher commissions than others, but his two-year average was $4,000 in commission for each sale he made.

One day Walt had lost some weight, and I asked him, "Are you on a diet?"

"No," said Walt, "I'm on a commission."

Walt's annual low goal for sales was 25 sold. Twenty-five sales a year equaled $100,000 in commissions and 30 sales equaled his high goal of $120,000.

"How do you eat an elephant...?"

Keep 'Em Bite-Sized, Not Super-Sized

Walt and Steve were good at breaking down the goal into smaller bites. After all, how do you eat an elephant? One bite at a time. Success by the inch is a cinch; by the yard it's hard. A journey of a thousand miles begins with a single step. You get the idea.

Walt set a monthly results goal of two banks per month for the first 11 months of the year, and then three banks in December. This equaled his low goal of 25 sales. His high goal was broken down as six months of two sales per month and the remaining six months of the year at three sales per month. Walt went a step further; he decided that every month by the 15th, he would have sold one bank. Here is a diagram of Walt's goals:

Low Goal: $100,000 in commission

2 sales per month x 11 months	= 22 banks
3 sales in December	= 3 banks

———————————————————————

= 25 banks @ $4000 per sale
= $100,000

High Goal: $120,000 in commission

2 sales per month x 6 months	= 12 banks
3 sales per month x 6 months	= 18 banks
	= 30 banks @ $4000 per sale
	= $120,000

Walt took one more step. He wrote all these goals down and gave a copy to his manager, his wife, and the CEO of the company. Why? He wanted to put pressure on himself to perform. And, boy, did he ever.

Steve's plan looked the same, but his average sale resulted in a higher commission. He had made $5,000 per sale in commissions the last two years, so he adjusted his goals appropriately. His sales looked more like twenty banks annually for his low goal and twenty-five banks annually for his high goal. He also included his mother on his distribution list of the written goals for a little added pressure.

Some people don't set results goals monetarily, and that's fine. Some salespeople set a goal to go on a winners' trip, to be among the top 10 salespeople, or to be number one in the company. These are all still results goals and require the same formula.

"Set specific goals to get exactly what you want."

The more specific you make your goals the better they are. Dave Waddle was an American athlete competing in the 800-meter-run in the Olympics. You may remember him, because he ran with a baseball cap on. He set a stated goal to run the 800-meter race in a then world record time of 1:51 (one minute and fifty-one seconds). He did it exactly, but he only won the silver medal. A Swedish runner had set his goal to win the gold medal, and he did. Set specific goals to get exactly what you want.

Visualize Success, then Crystallize It

My third summer on the bookfield selling books door-to-door, I decided I wanted to be the number one salesperson. My sales manager encouraged me to do this, and I am sure that he and all the other 25 sales managers were encouraging salespeople on their teams to do the same.

How do you know you can't fly? Have you ever tried?

This fact didn't even dawn on me at the time, but I realize that now. Before that summer started, I went through the following exercise. Let me tell you, it worked! I became the number one salesperson in the company.

The summer before, I had sold to approximately 1,000 customers. After crunching some numbers, I determined that my average customer bought roughly $40 worth of books. I then factored in the fact that the top salesperson the previous summer sold about $45,000 worth of books.

According to the numbers, to beat the top salesperson from the summer before, I was going to have to sell 125 more customers or raise my average sale to $45 per customer. I could have just worked one and a half more weeks in the summer and got the same results because I was selling about 80 customers per week. However, I didn't want to get back to school late, so that wasn't an option.

"It's crucial to put it on paper..."

Here is what my goals for that summer looked like:

Timeframe:	12 weeks
High Goal:	100 customers per week (average sale $45)
	= $4500 per week / $750 per day
Calculations:	12 weeks x 100 customers
	= 1200 customers with $54,000 in sales (which would be a new company record at that time)
Low Goal:	Beat the previous year's top salesperson by $1

It's crucial to put it on paper just as I did and visualize the goals. You see, although I set the goal to be number one – a noble and ambitious goal – I had to follow the same results formula to get to where I was going.

Over the years as a sales manager, countless salespeople have told me their goal was to be number one – but those weren't real goals. They sounded great and resolute, but there was no planning or crystallization to make the goals happen. As the poet Robert Browning said: "A man's reach should exceed his grasp, or what's heaven for."

I didn't set my goal to be number one "if" my car didn't break down – because it did. I didn't set my goal to be number one "if" I didn't get sick – because I did. I didn't set my goal to be number one "if" I didn't run out of sales territory – because I did. I didn't set my goal to be number one "if" my roommates didn't quit – because they did.

"I set my goal to be number one despite my circumstances."

Don't Stack

On the bookfield that summer, some days I was on track, and other days, sales were slow. This will happen to even the greatest of salespeople throughout their careers and that's OK. The important thing to remember is that this will, in fact, happen. So don't stack your results goals. If you don't get the results you want one day, one week, or one month, don't stack up your shortfall into the next goal period. Goals are designed to help you, and stacking can create a millstone around your neck that will sink you.

Stacking goals never works. If you have set an annual goal and you see that you're far behind six months into the year, just reset your goals. Trying to hit your initial goals becomes impossible and your goals have become a whip, not a dangling carrot. On the other hand, if you've already hit your annual goal six months into the year, you should reset your goal higher. Smart companies recast their budget six months into the year, either raising or lowering their forecasts and goals for profits.

That's all you are doing, recasting your goals for more motivation and mental crystallization.

Hold Yourself Accountable

That summer that I was number one, I told my sales director about my goal, and he reminded me of it every week. I went on to sell 1200 customers, sold my customers an average of $42 worth of books, and broke the sales record. Your goals can be written down and broken down, but you cannot skip the important step of communicating your goals to someone important. You do this to keep you on the hook.

That's why weddings are public, to keep you committed . . . or at least to try. Christians make a "public profession" of their faith to keep themselves held accountable. You have to put yourself on the hook if you want to maximize your mind's ability to get off the hook by getting the results to which you are verbally committed. Who you share your results goals with is up to you. The point is to share them.

You write your goals down not to stick them in a drawer, but to give yourself a visual image of what you want to achieve. The more often you look at these goals, the clearer their mental realization becomes. Goals are the initial push of the proverbial snowball down a hill that inevitably becomes an avalanche. Nothing on the face of the earth can stop it. Go through this goal-setting process and start your own personal avalanche.

Goal Tracking: Follow the Bread Crumbs

Setting goals is not enough. If it were, I could stop the goal setting process right now and end this book. Once they are set, you must track them.

I love legendary NBA basketball coach Pat Riley's book and the story of how he set a goal for each starter on the Lakers to be the best at their position. He posted the stats of the best player in the league at each position, and then he compared his players' stats to those top players as benchmarks. This posting was public, posted for all to see.

By the end of the season, he had the best players at every position, statistically speaking. And they won the championship – Riley's ultimate goal. That's the perfect example of setting specific goals and then tracking them each week. Not all of us will have a sales manager as good as Pat Riley, but we can track and measure our own results compared to both our activity goals and our results goals.

A Simple Sales Report

Most companies have a standard sales report form. The longer I train salespeople, the simpler I realize these reports should be. Here is what you should track each week – new activity, follow-up activity, and future activity. For example, it could look something like this:

Week Of:	New Presentations	Follow-Up Visits	Appointments Set Next Week
July 1st	3	7	4
July 7th	4	6	3
July 14th	3	8	9

If you want to track daily activity, then just expand your report. By tracking this activity, you know where you stand each week. You'll find that activity is a precursor to results.

You also need a simplistic report for your results because most results are measured in dollars. If you sell something that isn't measured in dollars, for example, if it is measured in units, then adjust the report from dollars to units to fit your company's tracking method:

Week Of:	Number of Sales	$$ Value of Sales	Year to Date Numbers	Year to Date $$
July 1st	3	$3,000	46	$46,000
July 7th	4	$4,000	50	$50,000
July 14th	6	$6,000	56	$56,000

Again, it's simple to expand this to daily results.

"It's hard to win if you don't keep score," said my first sales manager, Sam Johnson. I say it's hard to score if you don't know the score.

...or maybe you're at work and your manager asks you for another sales report.

From time to time, I meet a salesperson who says: "All my company ever wants me to do is fill out reports."

I'm sure that's true sometimes, but the truth is this: What could your company ask for that you aren't tracking yourself? The more you know about what you're doing, the more effective you'll be.

In Review

- The third foundation of a great presentation is goal setting and tracking.

- Set goals in at least two areas:

    1. Activity goals (like tracking the number of phone calls you make).
    2. Results goals (like your desired salary for the quarter).

- Break your goals down to avoid being overwhelmed.

- Avoid stacking your goals; rather, adjust accordingly to maintain your momentum.

- Have both high and low goals.

- Write your goals down! You have enough to remember already.

- Give your goals a specific timeframe for completion.

- Hold yourself accountable, and have an accountability partner.

- Track your goals with an easy-to-understand sales report.

"Sales techniques are really just good communication skills."

Chapter 10

Sales Techniques Are Not for the "Cool" People

No One Said It Would Be Easy

In building a fantastic presentation you must adopt equally solid sales techniques. Every great professional develops special techniques that are not natural. In tennis, no one naturally holds the racquet on the backhand like the pros. Golf requires unnatural grips and swings as well. Lawyers learn negotiation and questioning techniques that are not natural. If you're a religious person, you know sometimes your faith requires unnatural behavior. In the medical field it goes without saying that there is a learned behavior required.

Don't use the "It doesn't feel natural" excuse. Demand excellence of yourself, and this does not happen naturally.

The Voodoo doll is a good idea, but let's not forget the boxing skills, ok?

Sales techniques are really just good communication skills. Somehow techniques have gotten a bad rap because people classify them as "tricky". As long as you truly and sincerely believe the prospect will benefit from your product at the price you're asking, then there is no trickery. As long as there is nothing but truth, as you know it, in your communication, then there is no trickery. You must be the best communicator you can. Your prospects know you are not there to save the dolphins. Your goal with these techniques is to make it easy to buy.

Enthusiasm is "In"

Let's talk about some specifics that great salespeople use to make the sale. Enthusiasm is critical. Remember in our definition of selling that sales involves a transference of feeling. If there is no enthusiasm in your voice, there can be no real transference of feeling. Some consider women to be instinctively better at this than men. Men learn from an early age that it's not cool to be enthusiastic.

However, companies don't pay salespeople to get their "cool cards" punched. You're paid to make sales, and enthusiasm is important to that process.

Greg Daily is one of the most successful entrepreneurs I know and worth well over $100 million dollars. For more than 20 years I've always heard him answer a simple question the same way.

"Greg, how's it going?" someone would ask.

"Fantastic!" Greg would say. Every time.

Trust me, it's not always fantastic for Greg, but he recognizes the power of enthusiasm.

Enthusiasm is created in a number of ways. One way is through your vocabulary. When people ask me how I'm doing, I say, "Healthy, happy, and terrific!"

How do you answer that question? Start being enthusiastic in your answer to this basic question.

> *"If you act enthusiastic, you'll become enthusiastic."*

A second way to be enthusiastic is to use words that force you to be enthusiastic, words like:

- Great!
- Fantastic!
- Awesome!
- Wow!
- Magnificent!
- Amazing!
- Tremendous!
- Outstanding!
- Unbelievable!
- Wonderful!
- Excellent!

These words make you sound enthusiastic and are hard to say with any conviction without creating some enthusiasm in your voice. If you're not enthusiastic naturally, then focus on it, and practice using these words and others. If you act enthusiastic, you'll become enthusiastic.

"Motion creates emotion."

Get Your Body Talking

Another element of enthusiasm is body language. Motion creates emotion. In countless sales presentations, I've witnessed salespeople sit back in their chairs and talk to prospects from across the desk. These salespeople are working against themselves. If you're presenting to someone across the desk, get on the edge of your chair, lean forward, animate your gestures to the point of feeling a little ridiculous, and act enthusiastic.

If you're presenting to a group and they are all seated, then stand up! It's hard not to be enthusiastic when you're standing and talking, although I've seen some of my college professors and a few preachers pull it off. Just decide to get animated and get excited.

A common question salespeople ask me is this: "How do I sound enthusiastic?"

Remember that most people think about three times faster than they speak. I've noticed that enthusiastic and confident people speak faster. So, despite the misconception that "slow-and-steady" is always the best approach, speaking faster can make you sound more enthusiastic and hold a prospect's attention better. You can speak faster if you know exactly what you are going to say. This emphasizes the importance of a planned and well-rehearsed sales talk. The bottom line is this: Am I transferring my enthusiasm for my product to the prospect?

Nodding Your Head

Nodding your head is one of the most effective ways to get your body talking. With the simple nod of your head, you send positive vibes to your prospect. It also reinforces your own commitment to what you are saying and selling. Try this: Have fun with your friends by nodding your head up and down and then ask them to shake their heads "no." They will find it's very hard to do. This is the same positive impact you have on your prospect when you're nodding your head "yes."

"It is not unnatural to be enthusiastic."

Many times, your prospect will start nodding his head with you. This is a good thing. After all, it is hard to say "no" when prospects are busy saying "yes" with their heads!

Natural Comes With Practice

Allow me to dispel a myth believed by many salespeople: It is not unnatural to be enthusiastic.

I've heard salespeople tell me, "It feels unnatural." Of course it does at first, but what's natural about calling someone you don't know or knocking on the door of a total stranger? You must practice it until it becomes second nature to you. Then it feels natural.

Enthusiasm is not just a tone you portray in your presentation; it's a lifestyle. It works better if it's just a part of your life. It's not something you can just practice in your professional life. It is something you must practice in every aspect of life. Don't be the kind of person who brightens a room when you leave. Brighten the room when you arrive.

A good way to determine the level of enthusiasm you display is to measure your enthusiasm to your prospects' level of interest. It is very possible to overwhelm the prospect with too much enthusiasm. It's extremely rare, but if you're in a presentation and your prospect is actually fighting your enthusiasm, lower yours until they get on board with you. As a general rule of thumb, however, I'd much rather be too enthusiastic than not enthusiastic enough. When you fix dinner for your friends, it is much better to have too much food than not enough.

Look 'Em in the Eye

Eye contact is a technique that seems so simple and just plain common sense, but it shouldn't be taken for granted. When you meet prospects for the first time or any time, shake hands and look them in the eye. Catch their gaze for a moment. This builds trust and shows confidence on your part. No one buys from someone they don't trust, and confidence on your part is transferred to the prospect.

When you begin your presentation make sure that your visual aids don't prevent eye-to-eye contact, especially when you ask questions. When prospects ask you questions, look them in the eye. This is really important. When you ask someone a question and the person won't look you in the eye, you don't trust the response.

The Power of a Smile

A smile can often make more of an impact than a dictionary full of fancy words or phrases. It is one of the most simple, yet most powerful physical gestures you possess. I've often heard it said, "A smile is the nicest gift you can give someone."

I couldn't agree more. You should be smiling from the time you walk in the door until you leave. Like enthusiasm, this should become a way of life. We remember people who smile at us, and it can even make our day. Kim Kirkpatrick was the most popular girl in my high school. She wasn't the prettiest or the smartest, but she had a smile for everyone, and it always brightened me up to see her flash a smile my way.

My first summer selling books door to door, my sales manager, Sam Johnson, gave me a new technique to work on each week.

"Make sure you smile in every approach and presentation," he said during my fifth week on the job. "Smile all the way through the demo and don't stop smiling."

It seemed strange to me, but I was naïve enough to believe he knew what he was talking about. So I did it, and it worked. People bought more, and they smiled back. My mouth was actually sore from smiling by the end of the week, but I soon got over that and have never stopped. It's very hard not a return a smile. Try it. You can have some fun. People will wonder if they know you, or they'll wonder what you're up to.

You don't want to be like the man who got beat up outside the restaurant. When the police came, they asked the man, "Can you describe the man who did this to you?"

"That's what I was doing when he hit me!" said the victim.

A smile will disarm your prospect and make you feel better too. Ask yourself: "Do I like people who smile better than those who don't?"

Again, it isn't natural, but it's a skill that can be learned. Learn it!

Why crawl? I gotta dance!

In Review

- Every great salesperson needs an arsenal of solid sales techniques.

- Techniques are not trickery; they are really just good communication skills.

- Here are some essential sales techniques that involve your body movements and transference of emotion:

- Use enthusiasm. It is essential for the sales process, for that transference of feeling to occur. The following are ways to express enthusiasm - use enthusiastic words and use energetic body language such as nodding your head to convey enthusiasm.

- Appearing natural comes with practice. Make enthusiasm a part of your daily life and it will come across naturally to prospects.

- Maintain good eye contact as much as possible.

- Don't forget the power of a smile.

"Nothing gives prospects confidence more than hearing someone else they know bought the product and likes it."

Chapter 11

Even More Techniques for Building Your BEST Presentation

"Oh, They Bought": The Power of Names

The most powerful resource in selling is the third party influence. Names, names, and more names. Nothing gives prospects confidence more than hearing someone else they know bought the product and likes it. So, how do you introduce names, individuals, or companies to a prospect in order to get the desired effect?

In the book business, I read a list of fifty to a hundred names of people who had bought from me before I ever demonstrated the books. When the prospect identified the ones they knew, I made a comment or a mental note. Then as I gave my presentation, I used the names that had been identified, and I also used those same names in the closing process and in answering objections.

In the banking business, I learned quickly that banks don't buy anything without references. They believe the pioneers get arrows in their backs, not rewards. A bank doesn't want to be a pioneer in the banking world, but they do want references of banks that were pioneers.

Here is how I handled this mindset in the banking industry to successfully introduce ten different products that were new and relatively untested at the time. After I established rapport and did fact finding to create or find a need, I handed them a laminated sheet with a list of the banks in the area that had bought my company's services. As they looked at the list, I made a mental note of the ones they said they knew or at least knew of. And those were the names I used throughout the presentation.

"You cannot use too many names in a presentation..."

Don't Stop the Name Drop

You cannot use too many names in a presentation, and here is how I recommend names be used. First, use names to introduce a feature or a benefit. Here are two examples:

"One thing Bill King liked about the program was how easy it was to administer. Let me show you how that works."

"One of the benefits Bill King liked about the program was how quickly he could get started."

The other way to use names is to answer objections in the presentation before they are voiced. If price is a common objection you're hearing, then introduce price in the presentation like this:

"Now here's how we get paid. I bet you'll be like Steve Counts. He was surprised at how reasonable the program is."

In a few instances, prospects have told me during a presentation that they're just not interested in hearing who else bought. If your prospect appears genuinely disinterested in hearing other names, be wary of the use of names in your presentation. However, you'll find these instances will be the exception and not the norm, so don't let one prospect's objections sour you on the idea. Make it a point to use one or two names at every feature or benefit in the presentation.

This use of names works, but because it is work to remember the names and to work them into your presentation, most salespeople won't do it. Make yourself do this. Start with only one name and build it up to ten names and more. This technique will help every aspect of your presentation because of the trust and credibility it builds.

Know Your Enemy: The Competitive Advantage

Knowledge of the competition is essential to reaching the goals you set for yourself. When I was selling books door-to-door, I looked at every competitive product in every person's home I could find. It took some extra time, but like Zig Ziglar says, "You can't be too busy chopping wood to sharpen the axe."

When I sold products to banks, I subscribed to twenty-three banking publications, and I paid for them myself. Why did I invest so much time and money on looking at competitive products and reading trade publications? Two reasons: I wanted to know my competition, and I wanted to know my industry.

There is a reason that every great coaching staff in sports watches films of the competition. The great hitters in baseball watch films of the pitchers and pitchers watch films of the great sluggers.

It is impossible to find or create needs for a prospect if you don't know what those needs might be. You can get a real jump on the game if you know what's happening in your industry. I can't stress enough how the quality of your presentation will improve if you know what is happening on an industry level.

John was the top used-airplane salesman in America. After talking to him, I was convinced that he didn't know much about the sales process. But he did know the capabilities of every airplane on the market as well as every airplane that was for sale in the United States. He did his homework so that he could speak to his prospects with confidence, knowledge, and an ability to meet his customers' needs.

> *"If knowledge is not a talent, then it's a great substitute."*

If knowledge is not a talent, then it's a great substitute. When combined with skill and talent, it's unbeatable. Be sure you've seen your competitors' proposals, promotional materials, and (if he's any good) your direct competitor's name – the salesperson, not the company (duh)!

Bill Tomson was my competitor, now he's a friend. In competitive situations, he always wanted to go last in front of the prospect or group of prospects. After losing several sales to Bill, I caught on. From then on, I preempted that maneuver at every occasion. I either went last or asked for one last shot if I knew Bill's presentation was following mine. If Bill did follow me, I made sure the prospects were prepared not to make a decision until I had my last shot. I didn't lose to Bill anymore.

Never underestimate the competition. American Airlines told themselves Southwest Airlines was a low-cost provider. General Motors and Chrysler did the same. Now Toyota and Honda have moved ahead. Sears thought they could give up the low-end customers to Wal-Mart. Wal-Mart then drove Sears to the brink of failure and bankrupted Service Merchandise, a four billion dollar company with 375 stores.

How can anyone call themselves a professional if they don't know the competitors' products and sales strategies as well as they know their own? Don't accept defeat graciously, even occasionally. It forms a bad mental habit that it's OK to lose once in a while. It isn't.

Outsmart 'Em

Three stores on the main street in town stood side by side. They all sold the same type of merchandise. One day the owner of the store at one end put up this sign: ROCK BOTTOM PRICES.

This prompted the storekeeper at the other end to hang up a sign reading: LOWEST PRICES IN TOWN.

The owner of the store in the middle was thrown by these aggressive maneuvers until he had a bright idea. He put up his own sign, which proclaimed: MAIN ENTRANCE.

Like the owner in the story you must find a way to write "Main Entrance" on your product line or service. There is always a way to outsmart the competition.

Bite Your Tongue

Know your competition, but never cuss or bad-mouth them. Competition makes you better and ultimately helps the customers win. And, unless the customer is winning, ultimately none of us as salespeople will win.

Can you imagine Pete Sampras winning fourteen Grand Slam tennis tournaments without Andre Agassi or Jim Courier? Of course not! Your competition will drive you to new heights of performance and service.

Get Organized... and Give Yourself a Raise

Great presentations also come from having organized materials. I've actually been in several presentations with salespeople where the prospect was ready to buy, and there was no contract or order to be found. The salespeople would say things such as: "I gave my last brochure away yesterday, and I forgot my proposals when I left the house."

I've even heard: "Oh, I left my material at my last sales call."

Can you imagine a great attorney showing up at court to file a motion without the motion; or a doctor in surgery saying he left his scalpel at home; or a preacher saying he forgot his *Bible*? We would all find those funny, ridiculous, or impossible. But many times, that's exactly what salespeople do.

My friend, Keith Pitts, is the CFO of a large hospital chain, and he always says: "The devil's in the details."

Going without all your material to a sales call is like playing golf without all your clubs. Sometimes you need the four-iron to win the round.

If you're gone from your home or office for a day or a week, or even longer, make sure you have enough materials to get you back to the office or your home.

In Review

• Use names to build rapport and credibility with your prospects.

• Know your competition to help maximize your performance and achieve the goals you have set.

• Learn your industry well and know your competition.

• Stay organized! A messy salesperson is an inefficient salesperson.

Chapter

Getting in the Mood: The Buying Atmosphere

"Spectacular performances are always preceded by unspectacular preparation."

Spectacular performances are always preceded by unspectacular preparation. I so strongly believe that what you do before the actual performance in preparation is just as important as what you do in the performance that I'm spending time on the foundations of a great performance before getting to the specifics of giving a great presentation.

Let's discuss the concept of creating a buying atmosphere. The buying atmosphere is an environment where the prospect feels comfortable to say both "yes" and "no" to your product. It is an atmosphere where, unlike many sales situations, potential buyers do not have that fear of "getting sold" and instead can focus on determining whether the product or service truly fits their needs.

Buying vs. Being Sold

There is a natural resistance between prospect and salesperson. Some call it skepticism, healthy suspicion, or just plain mistrust. Most prospects are not saying to themselves, "Why should I buy?"

They are saying, "Why shouldn't I buy?" Understanding this is basic to understanding the psychology of selling.

Everyone loves to buy, but people hate to be sold. When I describe a product I've purchased and totally love, *I bought it*. When I purchased a product that didn't work out as I'd planned, *I got sold*. I don't even mind paying too much if I buy it, but I hate to be sold an overpriced product. This is the difference between a buying atmosphere and a selling atmosphere. Although you may start out across the desk from your prospect, your goal should be to mentally sit on the same side of the desk as the prospect in a counselor role as opposed to a sales role.

A single phrase or a few sentences is sometimes all that separates the creation of a buying from a selling atmosphere. For example, you walk into a retail-clothing store and the clerk runs over and says, "May I help you? We have jeans on sale today! Can I show them to you?"

When this happens, you become immediately defensive, and a selling atmosphere has been created. You reply, "No, I'm just looking."

You went into the store with some purpose in mind, or maybe you really just wanted to browse. But you did not come into the store to engage in the "selling process." You want to feel in control and buy what you want.

On the other hand, you walk into the same store and the salesperson walks up and says, "Hi, my name is Erin, and if you see anything you need help with, just let me know."

There, the beginning of a buying atmosphere has been created.

The question is: How do I create this atmosphere where I maintain control and yet the prospect feels in control? It certainly isn't easy. Millions of salespeople have taught prospects to expect a selling atmosphere.

There's a fine line between the prospect feeling controlled or being in control.

An old Italian man lived alone in the country. He wanted to dig his tomato garden, but it was very hard work because the ground was rock solid. His only son, Vincent, used to help him dig his garden every year, but Vinnie was in prison. The old man wrote a letter to his son and described his predicament:

Dear Vincent,

I am feeling pretty badly because it looks like I won't be able to plant my tomato garden this year. I'm just getting too old to be digging up a garden plot on my own. I know if you were here my troubles would be over. I know you'd be happy to dig the plot for me.

Love,
Dad

A few days later, he received a letter from his son:

Dear Dad,

Don't dig up the garden. That's where I buried the bodies.

Love,
Vinnie

At four a.m. the next morning, FBI agents and local police stormed the property and dug up the entire area without finding any bodies. They apologized to the old man and left. That same day, the old man received another letter from his son. It read:

Dear Dad,

Go ahead and plant the tomatoes now. That's the best I could do under the circumstances.

Love,
Vinnie

If Vinnie had tried to sell the authorities on digging up his father's garden, he would've failed, but because they felt in control, they gladly dug up that garden for Vinnie's father.

"Either Way is Fine With Me"

There are some specific things you can do to create this buying atmosphere. The first is to believe the phrase, "Either way is fine with me."

> *"It is not something you just say. You must believe it when you say it."*

Repeat the following statement to yourself and believe it:

It doesn't matter whether my prospects buy or not. It only matters that I help them make a decision about my product. I want them to buy, but I can't control that. I can only control my performance.

If you believe their final decision truly matters to you, prospects will sense that, and the "mistrust radar" will go up. If they believe you honestly don't mind either way, they'll be less suspicious and less resistant to what you say. Picture yourself on the prospect's side of the desk because ultimately that's where you must be to create a buying atmosphere.

Here are some great phrases to build a buying atmosphere into your presentation:

- "This may work for you. It may not. You'll have to decide that."

- "I wouldn't want you to get this product, item, program, unless you really thought you'd get benefit from it."

- "My job is to explain (show/demonstrate) this product to you and let you decide whether it will help you or benefit you."

Somehow you must let the prospect know that it is OK to say "no." It's not OK for the prospect to put you off, but it really is OK for them to say "no." The first step in creating a buying atmosphere is to allow the prospect to feel in control and get the sense that they can decide against a purchase if they want to.

I wouldn't want you to back up if you didn't want to.

First Impressions That Build Trust

The second step in creating a buying atmosphere is to cultivate an environment where the prospect trusts you. Unless you're presenting to someone to whom you're related or someone who knows you very well, you have to do something or say something that builds this trust.

"Your appearance communicates a message..."

Your appearance communicates a message about your trustworthiness to prospects. You've heard it said that first impressions are everything – you never get a second chance to make a good first impression. A prospect would probably not trust you in a ski mask and carrying a gun, so if you agree that there is an inappropriate appearance (the "ski mask and gun" look), then there must be a best appearance you can present as well.

The best advice is to dress like your prospect, or slightly better. In the banking industry, I wore suit-and-tie for sales calls. When I sold books door-to-door, I didn't wear a tie, but I also never wore a t-shirt and flip-flops. I tried to look acceptable to both the banker and to the housewife.

Just ask yourself this: If I were the prospect, how would I want the salesperson calling on me to look? Be critical of your appearance and try to improve it. Also ask yourself, does my competition look better than me? Be honest with yourself.

When it comes to your words, there are two very powerful things to use when building trust:

1. Other customers' names
2. Statements that put the prospect in control such as: "This may be a fit for you and it may not. That will be for you to decide."

The hardest part about making these trust statements is that old sales material, and even some new material, suggests that you must only make positive statements and always assume the prospect is going to buy. While it is true that you should always assume the prospect is buying and make assumptive statements, this should only happen after some level of trust and a buying atmosphere has been established.

Using Take-Aways

You may say one thing to the prospect to help them feel comfortable, and at the same time silently believe he should and will buy. The greatest discovery I've made in improving the quality of my presentation is the power of establishing a buying atmosphere with what I call "take-aways," phrases that literally take away the pressure on the prospect or the fear of getting sold.

It is crucial to eliminate as much of the inherent tension and pressure as possible. There is an entire mental process that begins in the prospect's mind from the first word you utter and continues throughout every stage of interaction. Therefore, much of the sales process is like an internal tennis match – back and forth – in the prospect's mind.

No matter what you're selling, prospects are silently asking themselves questions like these while you speak to them:

- "Will I actually use this product if I buy it?"
- "Will I get the benefits claimed if I buy it?"
- "What will my friends or business peers say?"

Prospects may give no outward indications as to their thoughts, but that doesn't mean they aren't thinking them, because they are. To alleviate these doubts and the stress the prospect is experiencing, you create a buying atmosphere by letting the prospect feel in control and by helping the prospect trust you.

The Zen of control in a presentation is to be in control while making prospects feel they are the ones behind the wheel. Any time you mention well-known names of people who have bought your product or make statements that allow the prospect to feel in control, you create a buying atmosphere and give them the feeling that they just sat down in the driver's seat.

Creating the Atmosphere for the... Atmosphere

Another part of a buying atmosphere is just that – the physical surroundings where you are talking to your prospect. It needs to be quiet place, void of lots of distractions. It should be comfortable, not standing up or out in the hot sun. It should also be non-threatening to the prospect. The prospect must feel in control, so sometimes it helps if you meet on the prospect's turf, or at least neutral turf.

When I have prospects come to my office, I make a comment about the atmosphere to try to relax them. For example: "I've asked you to come here so everyone in the office could gang up on you (Ha, Ha). Seriously, I won't ask you to make a decision today unless you want to. Does that sound fair?"

This does lots of things. It makes a joke out of what the prospect was already thinking, puts the prospects in control of the decision, and asks if it's fair. People love to be fair, and this gives them a chance to do that.

Part of a buying atmosphere is where you make your presentation, and part of it is who is in the presentation. If you don't have all the decision-makers present, you don't have a buying atmosphere, and the decision to buy simply cannot be made. This is because the buying atmosphere is also determined by the prospect's ability to buy.

In Review

- The goal of every salesperson should be to mentally sit on the same side of the desk with the prospect, to create a "counselor" atmosphere. This is the difference between a buying atmosphere and a selling atmosphere.

- Adopt a mentality of "either way is fine with me," as long as the prospect comes to a decision.

- Cultivate an atmosphere where the prospect trusts you. You can do this in several ways:
    1. Use take-aways and negative selling.
    2. Mention names of people they know who bought.
    3. Let them feel in control.

- Be aware of the environment around you – ensure it is conducive to buying.

"Memorizing your approach will raise your level of performance."

Chapter

Anatomy of a Sales Talk: The Approach

Once you are in front of the prospect, the sales talk is comprised of the basic outline as shown below. These are the elements that must be in the presentation – either specifically or implied – to make it complete.

These steps follow the initial approach and the setting of the appointment:

    I. The Set-Up
       a. Take Control
       b .Establish Rapport
       c. Find or Create a Need
       d. Create a Buying Atmosphere
   II. Product Demonstration
  III. Introduction of Price
  IV. Trial Close
    V. Close
  VI. Answering Objections
 VII. Close or Referral

"...now let's work towards 'ground zero'..."

Wouldn't it be great if it were that simple? Well from 40,000 feet, it is that simple. Now let's work towards "ground zero" by starting with the approach.

Fundamentals of the Approach

The beginning of each phone approach or initial approach should be memorized and written down so you can to refer back to it. Just as every young man practices his first call to ask for a date, salespeople should know what they are going to say and memorize it.

Some salespeople believe that they know the essence or the gist of what they are going to say on each call. My question for that mindset is this: "What's the difference between knowing what you're going to say and knowing exactly what you're going to say?"

Memorizing your approach will raise your level of performance. Remember, lightning bolt and lightning bug sound an awful lot alike, but their impacts are very different.

Phone Approach Example

Here are two phone approaches I taught when selling from the largest to the smallest banks in the world:

"Hello Mr. Parker, my name is Tom Black. I work with XYZ Company. Are you familiar with us?"

Whether they said "yes" or "no," I followed with the same response next:

"Well, XYZ Company provides software that helps banks attract new customers and maintain existing relationships. The reason I called is that I'll be in your area on Tuesday and I wanted to stop by and introduce myself and my company. Would you have some time on Tuesday morning?"

If you get a yes, then: " How about 9 or 11 a.m.?"

If no objection is given, you've got an appointment. After you have the appointment, you may try for a larger group meeting by saying something like this:

"Mr. Jackson, if there are other decision makers that you'd like to invite to the meeting, please do so. Is there anyone else that you'd like to attend?"

I was actually afraid to do this for a long time. I thought I'd lose the appointment, but what really happened is I got better appointments. Try it and I think you'll be pleasantly surprised.

Elements of a Great Approach

To make a consistently exceptional phone approach, here are the important elements:

1. Word-for Word. A plain and simple concept – write it out word-for-word.
2. Memorized. Memorize it or put it on a sheet of paper. You may want to laminate the paper.

3. Practice Makes Perfect. Practice it out loud several times. Think to yourself that you are practicing for the Academy Awards.
4. Plan out Answers. Write the answers to the most common objections down so you have word-for-word answers on the same sheet with your phone approach. No one is good enough to ad-lib a phone approach every time.

You know, I don't think there's ever a time you could call when I'd say it's convenient.

Here are some basic rules of thumb to keep in mind about the phone approach:

Keep it Simple. First, keep this in mind – the shorter the better. A one-sentence description of your company is all that should be given before you ask for an appointment.

Keep it Short. Second, you are not selling your product over the phone. In answering objections in a few chapters, getting around questions and objections during the phone approach will be addressed.

Keep it Upbeat. Third, you must be assumptive and enthusiastic when you ask for the appointment. One technique that helps me make better phone approaches is to stand up during the call. I find myself more assertive and enthusiastic this way. If you try it for ninety days and it doesn't work better for you, then go back to sitting on your better intentions.

Keep Track. Fourth, don't forget to track successes and failures on your phone approach so you can set goals to improve your batting average on future approaches.

If your approach is in-person, the same elements that apply to the phone approach are applicable to in-person approaches: Write it down, memorize it, practice it aloud several times, and write out the answers to the most common objections and memorize them.

These simple steps of preparation mean that you're ready to give a great initial phone or face-to-face approach to the prospect.

In-Person Approach Example

Here is an in-person, cold call approach I taught in the banking industry. This approach was targeted for the CEO or president of a prospective bank:

"Hello is Mr. Jackson here today?" (Do your homework and know the correct name before you go.)

Secretary asks, "Do you have an appointment?"

"No. I was in the area and I just wanted to stop by and introduce myself and my company. Is he available?"

At this point the secretary either calls to see if he's available or she asks, "What's it about?"

If she asks that question, the answer is:

"I work with XYZ Company, and we provide software to banks that help them attract new customers and strengthen relationships with existing customers. I'd just like to introduce myself and my company."

If the CEO comes out, greet him with:

"My name's Tom Black. I was in the area and I wanted to stop by and introduce myself and my company. I'd like to set an appointment to share some important information about our services. Would one day next week be convenient?"

The CEO invariably says, "What's it about?"

When this happens, I look at my watch and say:

"Have you got a few minutes now?"

If the CEO says "yes," you're in. If he says "no," then you set an appointment for later.

Now you know how to execute an approach in person, the dreaded cold call. People always ask me which is better – an in-person cold call approach or a phone call approach. The answer is I don't know.

It really depends on the industry, the product, and the salesperson. But whatever your industry requires, know what you're going to say and practice it. One sure way not to start is by asking, "How d'ya like me so far?"

I also wouldn't recommend the approach that the man in this story used. There was a very voluptuous woman who found herself in a sticky situation one day as she was boarding the bus, or attempting to board it. Her arms were filled with shopping bags, and as she went to step up on first step, she found that her dress was far too tight to allow her to step up.

A crowd was impatiently waiting behind her for their turn to climb on the bus. The woman had an idea. She reached back and, as inconspicuously as she could, attempted to gain a little reach in her step by pulling down the zipper just slightly in the back of her dress. It didn't help her at all, so she reached back again in desperation and pulled the zipper even further down, but it did no good. She simply could not step up.

Suddenly from behind her, a man picked her up and set her onto the bus. The woman looked back at him and exclaimed, "What gives you the right to put your hands on me? I don't even know you!"

"Well," the man explained, "after you pulled my zipper down the second time, I felt as though we were getting to know each other."

The old cliché "You never get a second chance to make a first impression" is a cliché for a reason: It's true!

"Create a sense of professionalism from the very first words you say..."

When you approach a potential customer, remember that this may be the first time this prospect has ever heard of you or your company. Think about how you want your company and your product to be remembered. Then plan your approach accordingly. When you create a sense of professionalism from the very first words you say, you'll be treated like a professional and, more importantly, you are one step closer to another sale.

In Review

- Make your approach the best it can be by performing these four fundamental actions:

    1. Write out all your approaches word for word.
    2. Memorize them.
    3. Practice them out loud and repeatedly.
    4. Plan responses to objections during the approach.

- There are also four things to keep in mind for phone, in person, or cold call approaches:

    1. Keep them simple.
    2. Keep them short.
    3. Keep them upbeat.
    4. Keep track.

Chapter

Anatomy of a Sales Talk: The Set-Up

The demonstration or initial sales presentation should follow the outline laid out in the previous chapter:

 I. The Set-Up
  a. Take Control
  b. Establish Rapport
  c. Find or Create a Need
  d. Create a Buying Atmosphere
 II. Product Demonstration
 III. Introduction of Price
 IV. Trial Close
 V. Close
 VI. Answering Objections
 VII. Close or Referral

Now that you've gotten past the approach, let's look at this outline step-by-step.

Let's Get This Demo Started

Step one is the set-up – what do you say to start your presentation? For every product I've sold or taught how to sell, the first rule for delivering a great opening statement is that it must be memorized. In the book business, once I entered a prospect's house, it was my goal to speak first.

Whoever spoke first was in control.

As I went through the front door, I said: "I've really enjoyed my work around here. Everybody's been so nice and friendly to me. Have you got a place we can sit down?"

This statement gave me control and also set the tone for the prospect to treat me like everyone else – "so nice and friendly." Next I remarked: "You probably know some of the people who've been getting things from me."

I'd name the most prominent people, neighbors, and relatives who had already bought from me. This built that needed trust and began to build a buying atmosphere. I then said: "What I'm doing is just showing something to everyone and then letting them run me off. You do have a big ole' broom you can use on me, don't you?"

This statement also helped to create a buying atmosphere, which made the prospect feel in control; they could feel free to say "yes" or "no."

Then I tried to find or create a need with questions like: "So where do you folks attend church?" Or, "What school do the kids attend?" Or, "How long have you lived here?"

> *"It's important to ask product-specific questions*
> *at this point in the set-up."*

When I sold *Bible* dictionaries, one of my product-specific questions was: "Have you ever read a word in the *Bible* you couldn't pronounce or wanted to know more about?"

With educational books, I'd ask: "Have your kids ever asked you a school question that you couldn't answer?"

The reason for asking product specific questions here is that once you've established rapport, you then try to find or create a need with questions.

In the banking services business, I followed the same formula. In fact, the fundamentals of this formula will work in most industries and for most products and services. As I walked into the CEO's office, I asked questions like: "How long have you worked here?" Or, "Where were you before that?" Or, "I noticed the fish on the wall. Did you catch that?"

These questions took control then established rapport. Once rapport is established, begin asking questions to establish a need. Then you can build trust by telling or showing the prospect other companies in the industry who are doing business with your company.

Finally, before I ever explained my product, I said: "This may be for you and it may not. Just let me know what you think."

Getting to the Specifics of the Set-Up

I gave the prospect the feeling of control, and I created a buying atmosphere. Again, I don't know of any product that is demonstrated in person where this formula doesn't work. To review, the steps for the set-up are:

1. Take Control
2. Establish Rapport
3. Find or Create a Need
4. Create a Buying Atmosphere

Now let's spend a little bit of time talking about each step specifically.

I. Take Control. The easiest way to take control is to speak first. Questions are a good way to control the conversation, especially if they're planned. Questions can be of a personal nature (careful – not too personal), or of a business nature.

"Establish the 'law of psychological reciprocity'..."

II. Establish Rapport. To establish rapport, you must find a common bond with the prospect. This is the definition of rapport at its base level. One reason you want to establish rapport is to establish the "law of psychological reciprocity" which says:

If you listen to me, I'll listen to you. If we have something in common, we will listen to each other. If we have nothing in common there is no reason for us to talk.

The second reason for rapport building is to build trust: *We have something in common so I can trust you.*

Finally, you establish rapport to answer the prospect's curiosity about who you are: *If I want the prospect to pay attention to me, I need to remove the questions about who I am.*

You can establish rapport by mentioning people that you know in common, talking about things that you do in common, or bringing up things that you believe in common. For example, if you've sold all of the friends of your prospect, you can use those names to establish rapport. If your prospect is a sports fan, you can discuss sports (this would be a good technique to use on me), and if the prospect has political items in the office, talk some light politics, and notice I said light politics.

Sometimes you may be in a situation where you find yourself looking for a way to establish rapport. Here's an idea that has worked for me over the years: If you're in someone's home or office, look for an item that is out of place. This is usually the item your prospect is most proud of, and there's likely a story behind it. That's why their good taste is overruled, and they have something placed in prominent view that doesn't quite fit in with the rest of the decor. If something is out of place, there's a good reason. I've found that this reason is a great source for rapport building, so look for it.

Believe me, Stan - No amount of sophisticated electronics or the Internet will ever replace the almighty Schmooze...

III. Find or Create a Need. At this point in the presentation, you've taken control and established rapport. Now you must find or create a need. Remember tongue-tied Charlie who sold toothbrushes? He created a need, when he said, "It *is* crap!"

In the banking business I ask questions about ROA (return on assets), ROE (return on equity), loan-to-deposit ratios, number of demand deposit accounts, and other questions. The questions diagnosed the prospect's bank in order to see if our product would meet the customer's needs. They were also designed to focus the prospect's thoughts exactly where I wanted them.

The CEO of a bank has a million things on his mind, and believe me, they are not all in the areas my product serves. That is why these questions should be pre-planned and memorized. This is true no matter what industry you are in!

In the book business, I created a need by identifying the areas that a prospective family's children had issues with in school. I found that parents would buy almost anything if they thought it would make their kids' lives a little easier. All I did was find that tricky subject or area of greatest difficulty, and that naturally created a need for the educational products my company offered.

IV. Create a Buying Atmosphere. To create that essential buying atmosphere, some specific statements must be made. Two things work to accomplish this: Showing the prospect the names of other people who have bought and making statements designed to help the prospect feel in control.

Here are some of those statements:

- I wouldn't want you to buy this product if it didn't help you.

- This may be something you want and it may not be. That is up to you.

- This product isn't for everyone. It may be for you and it may not.

- Whether you find this product is a fit for you or not is fine. But it's always good to know what others in your industry are doing.

When I first started using these "take-aways," I was afraid I would be encouraging the prospect not to buy. However, what I found was that it actually encouraged the prospect – and me – to have a more open and less defensive conversation. Try it. You'll be surprised!

Never Undervalue the Importance of the Set-Up

We've finished the set-up, so now you must ask yourself if your set-up has the elements just discussed. Countless salespeople skip this entire step or skip one of the four steps in the set-up process. They feel uncomfortable about asking questions, taking control, or giving the prospect the feeling of control. Most of the time, it is because the salesperson hasn't planned the set-up, memorized an opening, or simply lacks confidence to do the job right.

Whatever the reason, salespeople who begin a product demonstration without going through these steps are starting far behind where they could be and putting themselves at a disadvantage from the start.

"This is the essence of the set-up."

Can you imagine a doctor who came into the examination room, asked no questions, and then told you what was wrong? We'd call him a quack. In training, I tell new salespeople that the set-up is what a doctor does before he gives you the exam. Before he puts the rubber gloves on, he establishes rapport, finds a need, makes you feel comfortable – the buying atmosphere – and then does the examination. This is the essence of the set-up.

A word of caution: If you are still in the set-up and your prospect says something like, "Tell me what it is you're selling," you've talked too long in this phase of the presentation. That's why having it planned and enthusiastic is critical to your ultimate success.

In Review

• Here are the four elements of a great presentation set-up:

1. Take Control – by speaking first and asking questions.
2. Establish Rapport – by finding a bond with the prospect and by using names.
3. Find or Create a Need – by explaining how can your product help them.
4. Create a Buying Atmosphere – by giving them the feeling that they are behind the wheel.

Chapter

Anatomy of a Sales Talk: The Body of the Presentation

The Transition

Once the set-up is in place you can move confidently into the body of the demonstration. Here is a good way to transition from the set-up to the presentation:

"Let me show you quickly how our product works. We offer a software product that allows you to manage your commercial loans better and more efficiently."

In the door-to-door book business my transition was:

"Let me show you what everyone else has been so excited about. It's called the *Family Bible Library*, and it covers the *Bible* from Genesis to Revelation."

> *"Remember, ultimately you are headed for the buying line."*

Transitions like these are essentially one-sentence explanations of your product. The idea is to hold the prospect's interest and move you forward as quickly as possible. Remember, ultimately you are headed for the buying line.

What is the FBQ Demonstration?

Now it's time to demonstrate your product or service. There is a very basic but very precise format to the correctly planned presentation. It is called the Feature-Benefit-Question Presentation, or "FBQ". Here is an example:

Feature: "Our software gives you daily reports."

Benefit: "So you can always know where you stand."

Question: "That would be helpful, wouldn't it?"

If you have to write your own sales talk or tweak one you are already using, make sure FBQ is the general flow of the presentation. Every time I write a sales presentation for a new product, I write down features on one side of the paper and benefits on the other. On another sheet of paper, I write down questions that seal those benefits for the prospects.

"Here are some specific presentation techniques..."

I. Keep it Simple

Your presentation should be like a mini-skirt – long enough to cover the subject, but short enough to hold their interest. First, deliver your one-sentence statement of purpose:

"We sell exciting new software that allows our convenience stores to issue their own money orders."

Then add two or three sentences about the company and yourself:

"XZY Corporation has been in business for 15 years. We work with over 5,000 convenience stores in all 50 states. I've been with the company for 15 years."

With that simple step, you successfully and quickly remove the unspoken question of who you are.

II. Using Visuals = Good

I've heard it said that we retain fifty percent more of what we hear and see than just of what we hear. That's why I believe strongly in the use of visuals. I've used flip charts, PowerPoint slides, and even laminated sheets of paper given loosely to a prospect – whatever it is, show them something.

Flip charts or PowerPoint presentations are ideal because they give you an automatic outline for a planned sales talk. If you're selling a product like books, for example, the products themselves are your PowerPoint presentation.

You have to have a logical flow through the presentation. It must make sense, like a story or a TV show plot line. Your prospect is being led logically to the buying line.

It doesn't have to be long, but it does have to answer the most frequently asked questions about your product and explain the benefits.

It also has to pre-answer the most frequently voiced objections about your product because every great salesperson knows the best time to answer an objection is before it comes up. Once your prospect has voiced the objection, it has more power and authority because he's verbally expressed it to you. It is better that you answer it before he "wears it" than after he's gotten his ego into it.

"Once your prospect has voiced the objection, it has more power and authority..."

III. Load up on Questions

Your presentation must always be loaded with questions. Questions grab your prospect's attention. It is impossible to sleep while you're being asked questions. Second, questions show that you respect the prospect and are interested in their opinion; it makes the process interactive. Third, questions allow you to be in control. The person asking pre-planned questions is always in control of the direction of the conversation. Finally, questions lead the prospect in a direction toward a favorable "yes."

Can you imagine a presentation where you explain the product and get no feedback until the close when you say, "So, do you want one or not?"

That would be crazy! I've witnessed many presentations with very few questions, and inevitably there was absolutely no buying momentum on which to successfully close.

"Don't be afraid of a negative response. After all, you only need one 'yes'."

There are several reasons salespeople don't ask questions in their presentation. One is fear of a negative answer. Sometimes you need those negative answers to know what the prospect is thinking. Don't be afraid of a negative response; after all, you only need one "yes." Second, salespeople don't ask questions because they haven't preplanned their questions. It would be highly difficult to think of enough good questions in a sales presentation off the top of your head. The solution: Questions in the presentation must be preplanned.

Aristotle developed a method of asking questions called the "Dialectic". The theory was that if you answered his first question with a "yes", he could lead you to the conclusion he desired logically. One "yes" leads to another … and another … and another. This is true. We want to get a series of "yes's" from our prospects that lead to the really big "yes," but most sales are made emotionally and justified logically. So getting a series of "yes's" is good, but it doesn't guarantee the big one – the "Yes, I want to buy."

"'Yes' momentum..."

The best questions in your presentation are positioned so that they invoke that "yes." There is something psychologically appealing about your prospect saying "yes" over and over again. This is called "yes momentum," and you can only get it by asking questions.

IV. Vocabulary: Small is the New Big

I'm a believer in a large vocabulary, but simple words and simple sentences work much better in sales situations. Every time I hear a salesperson use a big word, I wonder: "Is he trying to impress the prospect?"

I'll bet the prospect is thinking: "Is he trying to impress me?"

Anything that puts a barrier between you and the prospect should be avoided at all costs. Besides, the really important words are small – words like love, trust, faith, and hope. Those are the kinds of words that will make your presentation better anyway.

V. The "P" Word: Price

Price is a word dreaded by both prospect and salesperson alike, but it is the inevitable conclusion of a sales situation. If a prospect wants your product, he knows he's going to have to pay for it. The ideal place to introduce price is somewhere near the end of the presentation. This is how I recommend you do that.

First, realize that everyone is wondering whether what you're selling is worth the price. If you told your prospect the price before you showed him the benefits, he'd be evaluating that number the whole time you were explaining benefits, and it would be less than the best atmosphere for selling. So wait until you have explained all the benefits before you introduce price into the presentation.

If you get the price question in the middle of the presentation, it can be a good sign (a buying sign) or a bad sign (a lack of interest in the product). If you are unsure which direction it's taking, you can say: "I am going to get to that in just a second, but trust me, you can afford it if you like it."

Or say: "It's less than a million dollars. Seriously, I am going to fully explain that in just a minute, but I'm sure you're gonna like it."

Once you've disclosed the price, it's more difficult to explain the benefits because all the prospect is thinking about is that dollar figure.

"Let's work on the price build-up..."

Assume you get to introduce the price when you want to introduce it, near the end. Then I believe you should have a price build-up. That means you use names, enthusiasm, and comparisons to justify your proposition.

In the book business, here was my price build-up, both simple and effective:

"Now Mrs. Jackson we've been playing a game with everyone out here. We've been asking them to guess how much something like this would cost. Mrs. Stevens guessed $200, and Mrs. Carter guessed $175, but actually they're just $99.95. That's for the whole set. That's reasonable isn't it?"

In selling products to banks, most products were sold on the basis of ROI (return on investment). So I used a sheet in my presentations that said: "This is how much you make from our program."

This sheet showed my prospects the ROI's from existing customers and specific ROI examples. I then had a second sheet that said: "This is how we get paid."

I finished with a question to seal off the price like this: "There aren't a lot of places a bank can get that kind of return on their investment, are there?"

Many times I've been in presentations with salespeople who don't use a price build-up and don't wait until the benefits have been explained to reveal the price. These are mistakes. They may not cost you the sale every time, but they certainly will some of the time. If your current sales talk doesn't have a price build-up, then put one in yourself.

VI. "How Does it Sound So Far?"

Another element of any good sales presentation is a trial close. I put a trial close in after the introduction of price so that the prospect has all the important information before I get to this point. You may decide to put it in before the price build-up, but it invites objections a little prematurely. However, I leave myself some room to maneuver if I need to keep selling. Here's my trial close for almost any product I've sold: "How does it sound so far?"

This was not the trial close I used in selling books because those were one-call closes, and that question would have invited the "I want to think about it" objection. This is something you don't want to do in one-call selling situations.

However, in selling products to banks the question was fine and allowed me to know where I stood. Usually the prospect would say, "It sounds pretty good, but …"

The "but" was a soft objection, and I dealt with it accordingly.

After the trial close I recommend you have one other fact about your product, then move into the close. The fact I tacked on for every banking product was: "It takes about ninety days to be up and running once you decide to do this."

It was simply a transition to the close if the trial close had gotten a favorable answer. This trial closing question – "How does it sound so far" – is one you can use with any product, so try it!

"Overselling is a dangerous path..."

Overselling is a dangerous path too many salespeople travel. Overselling means giving more information than necessary once a prospect's interest level has crossed the buying line. It is not usually done in the close; it occurs some time before that.

Here is a story that illustrates the danger of overselling:

There was a Catholic girl who was dating a Baptist boy. She really liked the boy, but she was afraid their families would never agree to a marriage because of religious differences.

"Get him to convert to Catholicism," suggested the girl's mother. "He'll never be more interested than he is now."

Sure enough, the boy started going to Catholic training. Things seemed to be going along great, and then one night the girl came home crying to her mother.

"It's over," she said. "The wedding's off."

"What happened?" asked the mother. "I thought you sold him!"

"I did, Mother," said the girl, "but I oversold him. He wants to be a priest!"

Here is what overselling looks like on the buying line chart:

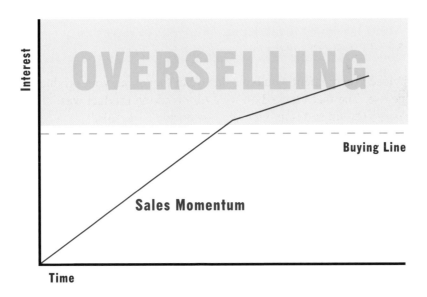

Anything said once you cross the buying line is overselling by definition. Every salesperson's goal should be to hit the buying line and to close at the same time.

One way to do that is with great questions that indicate where you stand. You will never get these if you're afraid to close, but the only way to keep the *momentum* going is with great questions that reveal how close you are to the buying line.

Let's see you try to get this up the hill with no momentum!

I've seen countless salespeople who were afraid to close. Know this: This fear of closing and call reluctance are the two biggest reasons salespeople fail. It is not natural to bring people to a point of decision, especially if you don't know them. But a planned close saves you if you just flow into it after you've introduced the price.

Remember you may not need all the steps of your presentation if the prospect is ready to buy.

I overheard this conversation at an airport in one of the airline lounges. Two men – we'll call them Man One and Man Two – were sitting together and obviously didn't know each other.

Man One asks, "So what do you do?"

Man Two responds, "I'm in sales."

Man One says, "Are you any good at it?"

Man Two replies, "Some people say so."

Now Man One says, "So sell me something."

Man Two responds, "I haven't got anything to sell you."

Man One looks around and says, "Well how about this ashtray?"

Man Two warms to the challenge. He says, "What would you want with an ashtray?"

Man One replies, "Oh, I don't know. I could put it on my dresser to hold my loose change since I don't smoke."

So Man Two asks, "Well what would an ashtray like that be worth?"

Man One shrugs and says, "Not over five bucks."

Man Two smiles and says, "Sold!'

You see, once you've established or created a need for your product and agreed upon price, it's time to move to the close.

In Review

• Use the FBQ – Feature/Benefit/Question – format for your presentation.

• The elements of a great planned presentation are:

    1. Follow the set-up with purpose of your product
    2. Give a brief history of the company and you
    3. Show the features and benefits of your product with lots of questions
    4. Execute the price build-up
    5. Use the trial close
    6. Add the additional fact

• Be wary of overselling.

"A close is neither a positive nor a negative response. It is simply the decision, the 'yes' or 'no'."

Chapter

The Close: The Moment of Decision

"Once you've told your story, it's time to get a decision..."

The close, on its most fundamental level, is merely a matter of bringing the prospect to a point of decision. A close is neither a positive nor a negative response. It is simply the decision, the "yes" or "no." Once you've told your story, it's time to get a decision, and this is the close.

Think about the close in this way: A young man and a young woman in high school went to a drive-in movie. The girl scooted over to the boy and gently grabbed his hand. She then put her head on his shoulder. He turned up the volume on the speakers as she sent a warm stream of air towards his ear. Now at this point, when he reaches over to kiss her, do you honestly think she will stop him and say, "I didn't say you could do that!"

No! She gave him all the buying signs. This story is the perfect example of the close – a series of questions that lead to the ultimate "yes." There is no pressure in this type of close.

Closing is not Improv

Some general rules about the close: First, the close should be memorized. That's right, word-for-word. It's just too important to ad-lib or wing it. Your close can generally be the same for every prospect, so that means it can be memorized.

Here are two closes for two products. The first is for a software product I sold to banks:

"Mr. Jackson let me ask you this – what kind of decision making process do you go through here in order to determine whether you would implement a program like this?"

The prospect answers this question, and this answer is irrelevant unless the prospect says that he is definitely NOT interested. Other than total disinterest, any other response at this point is fine.

The prospect may say: "I need board approval" or "I need to think about it" or "It's totally my call."

Whatever the answer, my response is the same:

"What most banks do is two things. They have me meet with other decision makers and influencers, and second, they call a few references. Would there be other people you'd like me to meet with and explain the program?"

Here is the first real moment of decision. Here the prospect has to make a minor decision that leads to the "big yes." If the prospect says, "No, I'll tell the board about it", that means he isn't sold yet, so stop closing and try to determine the objection and then answer it.

However, if the prospect said, "Yes, I would like you to meet with them," then ask the next minor question: "Could I do that today or some time this week?"

Here, pull out your calendar. This question combines two techniques for closing that we'll cover later in this chapter – alternate of choice and minor decision. Either option the prospect chooses is good for you, so this is another minor question that leads once again to the "big yes." If the prospect chooses either one, then ask the question:

"Who would you like in the meeting?"

Another Example of Superstar Closing

Here's another close, the close I used in the book business. It started like this:

"What everybody likes about the way I do business is that I am taking orders today and I'll be delivering your books at the end of the summer. I bring them back myself so you can make sure they're just like I told you they'd be. I'll send you a postcard about two weeks before I come telling you the exact day I'll be back (first minor question and decision). I am sure you'd rather have me bring them back than someone else, wouldn't you?"

If an objection is given, stop closing and show more features and benefits. If there is a "yes" response or no objection, continue with: "Could someone be home in the morning or evening if you had two weeks notice?" (Alternate of choice)

Get a "yes" here, and keep going: "Great, how do you get your mail here?"

At this point in the close, I'd pick up the order book and start to write. Once I had the address, I'd show the prospect the receipt with the price and sales tax and say: "Now if you can ok this, I'll send you that card." And with that, the sale was complete.

Alright, so would the 4th or the 5th of July work better for you?

Let's look at some closing techniques:

I. Assumptive Close. Both of these closes use some specific techniques you should use when closing. The first is called the "Assumptive Close". If the prospect answers all the questions with a "yes," they will give you a "big yes" at the end, and you're assuming the sale with each closing question. People usually don't say "yes", and "yes", and "yes", and then say "no."

II. Alternate of Choice. The second technique is the "Alternate of Choice". When both options are good, it makes it easier for the prospect to buy. We use this every day in real life, so it should come naturally. In the closing examples, the alternate of choice technique was used as a "minor decision" question that leads to the ultimate buying decision.

III. Your Body Says Yes Before They Do. The final technique is positive body action. In the first close, I pulled out my calendar. This is aptly called the "Calendar Close". In the second close, I pulled out the order book, and guess what? I called this "The Order Book Close" (very creative names, aren't they).

These three techniques should be used whenever you're bringing a prospect to a decision. It makes the decision process easier for the prospect and for you.

It's Not a Pressure Cooker

I've heard salespeople say, "I don't want to pressure the prospect" or "I don't want to trick them."

I have to laugh. You may be good, but it's doubtful that you're good enough to trick someone into buying by using these techniques. I never could. I've also heard people say, "That's too much pressure."

Those techniques aren't pressure. Here is pressure: "So do you want them or not?" That's real pressure.

What you're doing with the techniques we discussed is leading the prospect and making it easier to buy. In life, we do the same thing, and kids are especially good at this. We all ask indirect questions, which assume a "yes" to a bigger question.

"The End is Near!"

I loved to close when there was an impending event. You see it in advertising all the time. SALE ENDS MONDAY! We've all used these when we say things like:

"Mr. Jackson, our prices are going up tomorrow," or "Mr. Jackson, we're offering a discount on all programs that are bought this month."

When you can incorporate an impending event, then that event provides some real power to get a decision.

Lay the Framework

Many times in the close or pre-close, I set the time framework for the decision with a statement like this:

"Mr. Jackson, most bankers spend about two weeks doing their homework and then let us know whether they want to move forward. Does that sound fair?"

The prospect may push back, but whatever time framework you agree upon is better than none at all.

"He who talks first loses."

Wait

What about the old saying: He who talks first loses. I couldn't agree more. When you ask the obligating question, wait for the answer. Don't interrupt yourself. No matter how long you have to wait, just wait, and then wait longer.

In one close, I remember feeling like each second was an hour. I could actually see the tension in the air after I'd asked the obligating question. The silence was deafening as the banker just sat there looking at the contract. I'd explained it, he'd agreed, and now it was his turn to sign the agreement. He finally did.

I know that if I had started talking, the deal would not have gotten signed. Expect an answer to your obligating question, then wait for it.

Laughter is the Best Medicine

Humor can be good in the close. It's not the time to tell a story, but a witty remark can ease the tension:

"You know Mr. Jackson, no CEO who's ever bought this program got fired for his decision. Does that make you feel better? (ha, ha)"

In the book business, I liked to say:

"What most people do is give me a hundred dollar bill, and I bring them the change with their books." (The books were only $59.95.)

Find your own joke and stick it in your tool kit. It gives the prospect the sense that the decision is no big deal, and it brings you closer to the prospect as well. Who said you can't have fun with your prospect?

Learn Your ABCs: Always Be Closing

I've always heard sales managers tell their sales force to close early and close often. In the book business, after four summers and 20,000 prospects, I became very skilled at recognizing opportunities to close early. I've even had prospects buy after I'd read the names of the other people who bought. They never even saw the books until after they signed the order. You can definitely close before you planned in your sales presentation, but until you become an expert at reading interest level in your prospect, don't do it. Stick with the plan.

When new salespeople are in training, I often take them with me on sales calls to show them how to close. I'll say to a prospect:

"Mr. Jackson, I am very excited about our product service, etc. In fact sometimes I talk way past the point you may be ready to buy. If I do, will you just raise your hand?"

I've had lots of prospects raise their hands. Why? It creates a buying atmosphere and puts the prospect in control.

What about closing with resistance? Sure, I think we all do that from time to time. Here's my rule: When the prospect gives me an objection that I perceive as real, I give additional information before I close. You will be seen as a high-pressure salesperson if you close again after an objection without giving additional information that can help the prospect change his mind. Once you've given him additional information, then you can close again. In the chapter on answering objections, I cover this thoroughly.

In Review

- The close is merely a matter of bringing the prospect to a point of decision.

- The close should be memorized, just like the rest of the presentation.

- Here are three specific closing techniques:
  1. Use the Assumptive Close to gain "yes" momentum.
  2. The Alternate of Choice Close gives the prospect two good options, which makes it easier for the prospect to buy.
  3. Use some kind of positive body action such as the Calendar Close that makes it easier for the prospect to say "yes."

- The close is meant to happen naturally and without pressure. You are merely leading the prospect and making it easier to buy.

- When you ask the obligating question, wait for the answer. Never interrupt yourself out of a sale.

- Humor and laughter, when used tastefully and in moderation, can be good to ease tension.

- Learn Your ABCs: Always Be Closing.

*"When you take action, it's hard to slow
your momentum."*

Chapter 17

Special Tips on Closing

Closing within Group Dynamics

How do you close groups? Who do you ask to sign? There is an art to group clos-ing. In the banking business most decisions are made by group consensus.

One sale I am very proud of was to a large savings and loan company in Oklahoma. I presented our product to the marketing director, and he gathered the manage-ment of the bank for a group presentation. In the group presentation, the CEO was skeptical.

When it came time for the decision, I looked at the CEO and said, "Since Bill (the marketing director) is so convinced this will work, let's let him sign the agree-ment."

I proceeded to push the contract towards Bill, who did his part and signed.

What happened there? This is called neutralizing the negative influence. Many salespeople fail to identify the negative influence in a group situation and lose control of the group. One negative person in a group can mean failure and most salespeople have seen it happen. However, if you identify the negative influence, you can neutralize it and close with the positive influence.

"It only takes one "yes" to close the sale."

In the book business, the typical sales situation consisted of the husband and wife sitting on the couch together. I sat across from them on my sample case; six out of ten times the husband was negative while the wife was positive. I engaged both throughout the presentation, but when it came time to close I directed my ques-tions to the wife. One negative influence doesn't equal a non-sale. It only takes one "yes" to close the sale.

Gentleman Jim Corbett was asked how he became a champion. His response, "You fight one more round."

One skill that is important in closing a group presentation (12 people or less) is to know their names. When I sit down to make a group presentation I take out a blank sheet of paper and write their names down around a diagram of the table. Then I use every name a couple of times during my presentation.

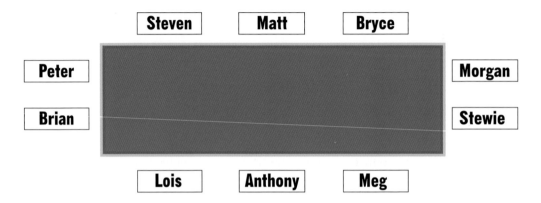

Getting Group Consensus

Closing the sale when more than one persons are present is more difficult than a one-on-one close. You must build enough of a group consensus to get them over the edge even if not all the group is positive. This is accomplished largely by the use of their names and recognizing who must be sold.

"Leadership is assumed not assigned."

Follow the Leader

In every group there is a formal and an informal leader – even in groups of two. One will be the leader and the other is the informal leader. Both of these leaders must be sold before you close. Leadership is assumed not assigned. Truthfully, there will be an "assigned leader" in a group, but there will also be someone who is assuming some degree of leadership. If you watch, that dynamic will make itself known quickly. Use this to help you close with the group.

Here is one of my favorite group closes. I have used it successfully hundreds of times. As the presentation draws to a close and the trial closing answers weren't a 100 percent positive, or if I had any doubt that I could close immediately after the presentation, at the end of the presentation I'd say: "Now what I'll do is step out of the room and let you make a decision while I wait."

I stood up while I was saying this so I'd get no resistance from the group. I kept moving toward the door, and as I walked out I'd add: "Take as long as you need, and if you have a question, I'll be right outside."

This close almost always worked to get a decision. Nine out of ten times with this close, the decision I got was a "yes." Don't forget that's your goal – to get a decision.

Back to the Basics of Closing

In closing situations, I've seen lots of salespeople launch their own torpedoes against themselves. Of course, the biggest barrier was not having a planned close. Get a sentence or two that you feel comfortable with, memorize it, and use it over and over again.

There was a man who owned vegetable stands, and he hired an immigrant to run one of them. The man couldn't speak English, so the man taught the immigrant to say three things – his canned close.

"First," said the owner, "the people will ask you 'How much?' You say to them, 'Two for five dollars.'

"Then they'll ask, 'Are the ones on the bottom as good as the ones on the top?' And you say to that question, 'Some are and some aren't.'

"Then, if they don't buy, they will say something like, 'I guess I don't want any.' And you say, 'If you don't somebody else will.'"

Later that day, a man walked up to the stand and asked for directions.

"Two for five dollars," said the immigrant.

"Is every vendor as stupid as you?" the man responded.

"Some are and some aren't," said the immigrant.

The man who had asked for directions was really mad at this point.

"I should just punch you in the nose!" he yelled.

"If you don't someone else will," said the immigrant.

Unless you want a punch in the nose, don't use a canned close like this one, but get a good canned close to use when it's time to close.

"Canned Close" Examples

Here are some ideas for a basic, good canned close. Use positive body language such as reaching for a contract, a customer information sheet, or anything you have to fill out. Then say:

"Now if I can just get some information from you we can get started."

This is a form of the "Order Book Close" that I explained earlier. Anything that gets you writing will bring the prospect to a point of decision. Another good close is:

"Let's go ahead and set a date now."

Say this while reaching for your calendar (electronic or paper). Again positive body language and the assumptive close are both used here. If you need to soften your closing questions so that the prospect doesn't feel railroaded, then add these words:

"Mr. Jackson, if you were going to do this, when would you start?"

Again, reach for your calendar as you say this. Or say:

"Mr. Jackson, if you were going to move forward, we need to set a date. Let's take a look at our calendars."

Out of thousands of salespeople at Morgan Stanley Dean Witter, my stockbroker is always among the top one hundred. Here's her simple close: "I need to get your current account information in order to move your account."

Then she starts writing. It is a classic order book close that moves millions of dollars under her control. Have a canned close, and if you plan on closing more than once, you also need to have more than one obligating question.

Self-Built Barriers to Closing

I've interviewed thousands of people for sales positions, and there is one question I like to ask: "What is your current closing question?"

I've found only about one out of every hundred actually have a canned closing question. No wonder they're looking for a job. I've never understood why something so obvious is missed by so many.

Salespeople also set barriers up for themselves through failure to use positive body language. When you take action, it's hard to slow your momentum. At the moment of decision, the prospect has doubts and fears, but your confidence can overcome this many times. A prospect who is teetering on the brink of a "yes" can be tipped favorably with your positive body action. Reach for an order book, a calendar, or your laptop, anything that physically assumes the sale is closed.

Well guys, I just kept trying and trying, and then SUCCESS!!

Another barrier that salespeople place in their way is not knowing when to close. At the end of our discussion on the presentation, the concept of overselling was introduced. Far too many salespeople oversell and never close.

"If you're repeating yourself, it's time to close."

Here's my rule of thumb: If you're repeating yourself, it's time to close. Don't repeat yourself. It is proof of every flaw we've discussed – no planned sales talk, no planned close, no confidence, no salesmanship in general.

One of the greatest salesmen I know, a man worth several hundred million dollars, called to ask me for a political donation. He told me his whole story twice and never actually asked for a specific amount. I gave him a thousand dollars so I wouldn't have to hear the story a third time. It just goes to show you that even great salespeople can be ineffective if they don't use the tools of the trade.

However, I will add this: That man did get a donation, principally because he called. It's good to remember what Woody Allen said, "Ninety-five percent of success is showing up."

It seems to me that many salespeople invite the stall into both their presentation and their close by how they answer the customer's questions. For example, the prospect says, "Do you have some information you can leave with me?" The average salesperson says, "Yes, and when I get done I'll leave you some brochures."

The great closer says: "Yes, but I am going to give you all the information you need to make a decision today. You'll know when I get done whether this meets your needs or not."

Here's another example. The prospect asks, "Do you have some references I can call?"

The average salesperson's response would be, "Yes, I'll leave you some when I am done."

The great salesperson says: "Yes, in a moment we can look at some reference letters together."

Both responses from the average salesperson told the prospect indirectly that they did not have to make a decision, but the responses given by the great salesperson let the prospect know indirectly that they were expected to make a decision. Your demeanor and the way you answer prospects' questions will also help you close.

In Review

- When closing a group, you must neutralize the negative influence. One negative influence doesn't equal a non-sale. It only takes one "yes" to close the sale.

- Build enough of a group consensus to get them over the edge even if not all the group is positive.

- Know the names of the entire group, and then use those names throughout your presentation.

- There is always a formal and an informal leader – even in groups of two. If you watch, that dynamic will make itself known, and you can focus your close on these leaders

- Get a sentence or two that you feel comfortable with, memorize it, and use it over and over again.

- Avoid "Self-Fired Torpedoes" to closing by following these rules:

  1. Use positive body language. When you take action, it's hard to slow your momentum.
  2. If you're repeating yourself, it's time to close.
  3. Your demeanor and the way you answer prospects' questions will also help you close.

*"Is the prospect objecting or just searching
for more information?"*

Chapter 18

Objections: Now the Work Begins

The sale starts when you hear an objection. Up to that point, you're really just exchanging information. It's at the point of objection that a salesperson's work really begins.

I worked with one salesman, Jim Samuels, who said he could sleep through the presentation, but he woke up for the close and to answer objections. That analogy is a bit extreme, but the point is a good one. You must prepare yourself to re-close two, three, four, five, or twelve times after each objection, and you must prepare yourself to determine the real objections from the questions.

Is the prospect objecting or just searching for more information?

Objections are Buying Signs

Every question is not an objection and every objection is not real. Every real objection is not an objection to buying and every objection is not spoken. Have I confused you? I think I confused myself. First, we need to identify types of objections and differentiate them from questions.

All Questions are Not Objections

When a prospect asks a question that may be interpreted as a potential objection, answer the question as directly as possible. I worked with a great salesperson who believed every question was the beginning of an objection. So, instead of answering the question directly, he answered the anticipated objection, and he and the prospect ended up frustrated. And it frustrated me watching him. Don't try to preempt the objection. Don't try to anticipate the objection. Just answer the question.

The one exception I make to this – the only one – is if I am going to cover the question that was asked in my planned presentation. Then I might say: "I am going to cover that in just a second, but let me explain this first."

Other than that, I answer the question. For example, if the prospect says, "Has anyone ever cancelled your program?" I respond with: "Sure we have cancellations, but let me show you this …"

"Most of the time questions are really buying signs."

Real vs. Unreal Objections

Real objections are different from questions. The best time to answer an objection is before it comes up. Translation: The answers to objections should be built into your presentation.

In the book business I did not come back to any house a second time once I gave a presentation. The expected objections were, "I want to think about it" or "Can you come back and show my spouse?" So in anticipation of those objections, in the set up, I'd say, "Since I am only able to stop at every house once, is there anybody else at home we should show these to?"

"I answered the objection before it ever came up."

There is the spoken objection, and it can be both real and unreal. In the banking world, the unreal spoken objection we classified as a "stall." Here's an example that I'll use later on in this chapter: "I'd have to ask the Board of Directors about it."

What the prospect was really saying was, "I am not sold, but I don't want to tell you my real objection."

Most bank CEOs could make a decision about anything I was selling, so that objection was not real. It was just a stall, and there will often be an objection voiced that is not really an objection.

What is the real voiced objection? Here is a perfect example: In the banking business, prospects would say, "We're in the middle of a merger and I can't make that decision now." That was a real objection.

The Unspoken Objection

The most interesting objection is the unspoken objection. The prospect is keeping a secret from you. It may be real; it may be illusionary; it could be almost anything. For the salesperson, it is the most frustrating. But it can be dealt with, and I'm excited to share with you how to do this.

I want you to have this attitude when you hear an objection: *Now the work begins because I know the answers better than the prospect knows the objections.*

When the prospect voices an objection, let's assume that it's not a real objection – it's a stall.

First, acknowledge the objection – and remember in your mind that you believe this is not a real objection. The best and only way to do this is respectfully. Even when you know exactly what your response is going to be, pause first, and then answer.

This is applicable to real life, not just in the selling world. If one of your friends expressed a real concern to you, you would think about it a moment and then speak. This distinction is important.

Amy Golden went to Brown University and graduated with Honors. She was accepted to both Harvard's and Kellogg's MBA programs. She was the smartest salesperson I've ever worked with. She was attractive, she knew our product, and she knew our sales presentation better than anyone else. And yet, she was a mediocre performer. Her numbers were always just OK.

I watched her on a few sales calls and immediately saw the problem. Before the last word of the prospects' objections even left their mouths, she was answering them. She was smarter than the prospects, and they could sense it . . . feel it. There was no respect, no acknowledgement. When Amy realized what she was doing, she changed and became a top producer.

Give Credit Where Credit is Due

Once you've respectfully listened to the objection, you must give the prospect the answer. A word of caution here: The more credibility you give the objection, the more credibility the prospect will give it. Therefore, if you believe the objection is less than sincere, don't give it much credibility.

Here is a good response to the "I need board approval" stall I introduced at the beginning of the chapter: "I know how you feel. I think a lot of bankers who've bought our program felt the same way. One feature that I forgot to mention is this …"

After responding, explain another feature or amplify one that was already mentioned, and then close again. If the same objection is given a second time, answer it.

This response acknowledges the objection, lets the prospects know that you understood how they feel, and tells them that they are not alone. It then lets the prospects know that many other people have bought despite this objection. Then, the program is resold so that you can close again. Remember, you aren't allowed to close again without giving the prospect some additional information. If you do, you deserve the title, "High Pressure Salesperson."

Now, don't jump to conclusions - I'm just a common cold.

It is surprising how many prospects will not repeat their objections a second time – and that's because those objections are really just stalls. The stall is just that – stalling because of a hesitation or unwillingness to come to a decision.

It has probably worked on dozens of other salespeople, but it doesn't have to work on you. In order to treat the stall as I've described, you must be prepared for it. You must have a specific feature that will illustrate a benefit ready to show and explain to the prospect when the stall is given.

The steps to overcoming a stall are:

    I. Acknowledgement
    II. Additional Information (Feature/Benefit)
    III. Second Close (Obligating Questions)

The important thing is to have something ready. In the book business, this additional information was another section of the books I sold with questions that illustrated benefits. In the banking world, I used actual case studies of the banks I worked with and demonstrated how our program was working for them.

The Second (Third, Fourth, Fifth ...) Close

To be prepared for this approach to answering objections you must have a new obligating question or series of questions. In selling to banks, my second close was: "Mr. Jackson, if you implemented our program, how soon would you want to start?" (Reach for the calendar or open it up.)

Alternate of Choice

Another question I used was: "Who will be in charge of the program, you or someone else?"

This technique is called the "alternate of choice." In the door-to-door book business, my second close looked like this: "Like I said, I'll bring the books back myself at the end of the summer, or I have a set in the car if you want to get them today. Would you just as soon get them today as to wait?"

Again, this is an example of the alternate of choice closing technique.

If the prospect repeats the stall a second time, you must answer the objection as if it were a real one. Chances are, it is – and you simply misjudged the prospect's sincerity the first time.

Feel, Felt, Found

The real spoken objection – the Grand Poobah. For this objection, use the technique that's been taught by all the greats for at least fifty years: Feel, Felt Found.

I don't know who labeled it that – it may have been Zig Ziglar – but before I ever heard that label, my sales managers at the Southwestern Company were teaching me the concept. Now I've taught it to thousands of salespeople as well.

It starts with acknowledgement of the objection: "Mr. Jackson, I know how you feel. Other people in your same situation have felt the same way. However, here is what they found."

Then answer the objection. You can make this answer much stronger through the use of names and specific examples. In place of "other people", use real situations and real people the prospect knows: "Mr. Thompson, Mr. Stevens, and Mrs. Carter all felt the same way before they bought. Here is what they found."

The third party influence is powerful here, just as it is in the approach, the set-up, the presentation, and the close.

The Buying Atmosphere Revisited

When you answer an objection, you must not sound like you're in control, even if you are – and you should be. You must think to yourself:

> *"I am sitting beside my prospect, not confronting him..."*

I am on the same side of the desk as my prospect. I am sitting beside my prospect, not confronting him with the fact that his feelings are wrong, immature, or just plain stupid.

Once again we must create a buying atmosphere. You can accomplish this by restating the objection in this way: "Mr. Jackson, I wouldn't want you to do this if it were too expensive. However, here's what other bankers like Mr. Carter found…"

When you tell your prospect you wouldn't want them to buy your product if it was not right for them, you gain credibility. There is a natural tension between salesperson and prospect, and when you say this, it reduces this inherent tension, and actually makes the tension work in your favor.

Negative Selling

Many times after my response to an objection, I heard a prospect say something like this: "No, it's not that. It's just that…"

If you have the courage and discipline to use it, you will amaze yourself by using a technique called 'Negative Selling.' Here is an example of that technique: "Mrs. Jackson, I wouldn't want you to get it if you couldn't afford it, but it's like Mrs. Jones said …"

You answer the objection by letting other people be the "bad guys." It is very hard to argue with a story. Prospects can deny your opinion, but they can't deny what really happened to a peer or friend. They can't fault you. After all, you don't want them to buy unless it's in their own best interest.

In the book business, the prospect would say, "I just don't know if my kids would read them", and there was never a truer or more sincere objection. My answer was not, "Get them anyway. I need the commission."

Instead, my answer was: "Mrs. Jackson, I know how you feel. Most parents like your neighbors, the Carters and the Thompsons, felt that way too. I wouldn't want you to get them if your kids wouldn't use them. Here's what Mrs. Thompson and Mrs. Carter both said…"

That's how a great salesperson answers the real spoken objection.

Objections Don't Have to End the Sale

One summer on the bookfield, I called on Mrs. Craighead of Farmville, Virginia. She was an older woman, and her family was grown. I showed her a *Family Bible*, and she loved it. When I told her the price, I thought she was going to throw me out the door. Then I learned this very important point: Every objection does not equal a no-sale.

Mrs. Craighead shook her head and said, "That *Bible* is just too expensive."

But then she paused for a minute and added, "But I've always wanted a nice *Family Bible*."

Well, I got her check, and she got her *Family Bible*.

"Not every objection is a reason not to buy."

In Review

- The sale really starts when you hear an objection – up to that point, you're just exchanging information.

- You must determine whether the prospect is objecting or just searching for more information.

- To successful salespeople, objections are just buying signs.

- The best time to answer an objection is before it comes up. Translation: The answers to objections should be built into your presentation.

- The steps to overcoming a stall are: Respectful Acknowledgement, Additional Information (Feature/Benefit) and Second Close (Obligating Questions).

- For the real spoken objection use the Feel, Felt, Found technique.

- When you answer an objection, you must not sound like you're in control – if you can do this, you will gain credibility.

- By using the 'Negative Selling' technique, you answer the objection by letting other people be the "bad guys".

- Every objection does not equal a no-sale, and an objection should not be interpreted as a reason not to buy.

Chapter 19

More Tips on Objections

The Buying Ritual

Many people have something called a "buying ritual." Go to the grocery store and watch people pick up the same item two or three times before they put it in their carts. Why? They have a ritual to their purchasing. They are going to buy Jiffy Peanut Butter, but they are still going to look at it several times and examine other brands as well before they commit to it. Sometimes people have to object just to fulfill their buying ritual.

When someone buys your product, and you pat yourself on the back for handling the objection so well, realize that the prospect was probably going to buy your product all along and was just making you go through their buying ritual with them. Sometimes the prospect is also just testing your commitment to the product and the process. They intend to buy, but they want to make sure you deserve it.

These rituals are very difficult to detect, and if you make a mistake, you'll likely lose the sale. So I say, why bother trying to determine if they have such a ritual – just treat it like a real objection and see it as practice for the really tough ones.

The Deadliest Objection is Never Uttered

The last type of objection is the one that is unspoken. You know intuitively that the prospect is not telling you the real deal. You just can't get the prospect to talk to you, or the objection doesn't make any sense. In either case, you need to invite the objection. Yes, invite it.

This is done through a very direct question that gets you to the truth behind the prospect's hesitation. To get the full benefit of this, realize where the prospect is mentally and where you may have been in other similar sales situations when you were the prospect.

The reason the prospect is not forthcoming with the objection is because he doesn't feel comfortable telling you. For some reason, he is not telling you the real deal. Your progress comes to a screeching halt, and you can go nowhere in the sales process because you don't know where the prospect is.

Now is Not the Time to Tiptoe

So, how do you get there, to the point that the prospect feels comfortable enough to give you his real objections? No matter what I am selling, it seems there is a time at the end of the presentation when I am packing up. Obviously if I haven't answered the hidden objections, it's time to wrap it up and pack it up. At that time, the prospect's defenses are the lowest they will ever be in the sales process. The prospect has "won," and he is beginning to relax. The defensive wall is coming down.

This is when I say: "Mr. Jackson, what is it that bothers you most about my product (service, etc)?"

Another example: "Based on what you told me, I can't see why you wouldn't want to do this. What am I missing?"

These very direct questions at this precise moment often reveals the real objection. If it works, you can then pause and begin reselling. No one said you couldn't unpack if you can reengage the prospect. Once you've gotten the real objection out, you can answer it. Use the same method described for the real spoken objection – the feel, felt, found technique, the use of names, and third party examples.

Isolate the Real Objection

When it comes to answering any objection, a good idea is to isolate the objection. In the banking world, I often heard bank CEOs say, "I need board approval."

So I would know if this was a real objection, I'd isolate it like this: "Mr. Jackson, if it wasn't for the Board of Directors, is this something you'd definitely do?"

If they said "yes", the next question was: "Well then, let me ask you this, does the Board usually approve the things that you strongly recommend?"

Whether the answer was "yes" or "no", I'd say: "When is the next board meeting?" (I'd check my calendar) What I'd like to do is be there that day. If you want me to present the program to the Board, I'll be there. If you don't, I'll just be there to answer any questions the Board has about the program. I can even just wait outside while you meet, and just be here in case the Board has a question. How does that sound?"

Now, if the prospect has agreed to all of this, then they are serious about buying, and you have isolated the real objection. If you get a balk or a stall anywhere in this part of the process, that means you have not found the real objection.

The banker may then say, "I can handle everything with the board. It's really just a rubber stamp."

I'd say, "Ok, but Mr. Jackson, let me ask you this, what do you think the Board's objection might be?"

This is inviting the real objection yet again. Whatever the banker says the Board's objection could be is probably the prospect's real objection that he never told you. Prospects are funny like that.

So what if the hat looks a little funny? The world could use a few more laughs...

Prospects Sure Do Like to "Think About It"

Here are some answers to common objections that sales organizations I've worked with have used. The objection I hate the most no matter what I've sold is: "I want to think about it."

I hate this and yet I've told salespeople trying to sell me something this very objection – duh. Here are some answers to this, and again remember to memorize a couple of answers to each objection so you have your tools ready:

"Mr. Jackson, I know how you feel. Lots of our customers have felt the same way before they bought, but here's what they found. Mr. Smith said this, "I'll never know more about the product than I do right now, and I guess I have all the information I need to make a decision." One thing I want to mention is…" (Now resell your product then use your second obligating question). So what I'd like to do is get some information from you and get started." (Reach for something you need to fill out and complete the sale.)

Here's another answer to the "I want think about it" objection:

"Mr. Jackson, I know how you feel. A lot of our customers felt that way before they bought. Usually when a customer tells me they want to think about it, that means there is some problem with the product, service, etc they want to think about. Do you mind me asking what that might be?"

This is a more direct approach that "invites the objection", the real objection, and then you can better deal with it.

I'm not Gonna Pay That! The Price Objection

Another objection most salespeople hear in their careers is the price objection. Most customers don't say the price is too high for the product or service you're selling unless a competitor is involved, so there really are two types of price objections:

1. I can't afford it.
2. Your price is higher than the competitor.

Both are price objections but very different. Let's start with the first one. The prospect is really saying, "I don't want to trade my money for the value I see in the product." If you've done a good job qualifying your prospect, you know they can afford it.

I say: "Mr. Jackson, I know how you feel. A lot of people who've bought our product felt the same way at first. However, here's what they found. Although the initial investment may seem high, the long term rewards are tremendous…"

I then explain the benefits and ask the closing question: "Based on that, Mr. Jackson, I'd like to go ahead and get started (This is said as you are reaching for your order book). Can you give me some basic information?"

Another more direct approach is: "Mr. Jackson, I know how you feel. A lot of people felt that way before they bought. Mr. Stevens said, "It's not that I can't afford it; it's more that I am not sure it's worth it." Here is why he bought: He thought of the purchase price as a one-time pain that would bring years of pleasure. You know, we have customers that… (Tell your story and the obligating question). With that in mind, I'd like to get your order (Reach for paper). Can I get some basic information from you?"

There are lots of catch phrases when it comes to price. Here are a few:

- "Mr. Jackson, most of us spends that much on _____ each day, week, or month."

- "Mr. Jackson, as hard as you work, you deserve this."

- "Mr. Jackson, I'd rather explain the price once than explain the quality of the product for its life."

You can think of them as well as I can. Write yours down and memorize them. Once I loved a pair of lamps, but they were very expensive. I was about to pass on them when the salesperson said, "It won't change your lifestyle will it?"

I told him "no," but I just hadn't ever spent that much on lamps.

The salesperson picked up the lamps (positive body language) and said, "I am sending these home with you," as he walked to the register. He closed on resistance with a power question. Get yourself your own power questions!

Your Price is Higher

How about the objection that the competition's price is cheaper? Simple translation: Your price is too high. Well, to that you say "feel, felt, found," and then your answer: "Mr. Stevens found that on an apples-to-apples basis, we were actually a better value." (Don't say cheaper!)

Or: "Mr. Stevens found that although the initial price was higher, the long term costs were actually lower. Here's how ..."

Don't say: "Well, I guess my competition knows what his product is worth."

I've actually heard salespeople say that. Here are some other thoughts when this objection comes up:

- "What is more important to you, price or quality? Don't you want both?"

- "If the prices were the same would you choose our product?"

- "Do you feel like both products are equal except for the price?"

These approaches isolate the objection so you can answer it, or it lets you know the real objection.

My last piece of advice about answering objections at the close of the sales presentation is to memorize answers to the most common objections and use them.

Objections Don't Just Happen at the End

There is another place you will hear objections – in the approach. Over the phone during your initial approach is a good place for the prospect to get rid of you. I've noticed over my career in selling lots of different products that prospects have their own unique points of resistance in the sales process. The hardest doors to get in were the easiest sales. They had no sales resistance and they knew it, and that's why they were so tough in the approach.

Other prospects will listen to every salesperson only to say, "We'll think about it" or "I have to talk to someone else." Some will even sign an order thinking they can cancel later.

What Are You Selling?

It is important to be prepared for an objection in the approach. Usually this objections is, "What are you selling?" in one form or another. You can't ignore this objection; but you can be less than direct.

For example, use this in response to that objection: "Mr. Jackson, It's a program designed to increase fee income, cross-sell your services, and improve retention. (No Pause) Like I said, I'll be in your area on Tuesday. Would 9 or 11 work for you?"

I answered the questions and closed for the appointment. The phone approach is designed to get the appointment, not sell the product. Of course, if you are in telemarketing, that does not apply to you, so just keep giving your sales talk.

If you're going for the appointment, this is how you do it. In person, if the prospect says, "What are you selling?" you do the same thing.

In the book business, I said: "What I'm doing is showing something to all the families with children. Your children go to Greenwood Elementary, don't they?"

The prospect says "yes" and I continued, "Fine, may I come in?" (And I wiped my feet as a positive body action).

You Need to Speak to Someone Else

Another phone objection I often heard was, "You need to see someone else."

Here's my answer to that: "Fine, Mr. Jackson, I'll be glad to meet with whoever you want me to. (He's won and you've created a buying atmosphere.) However, my experience suggests that I meet with the CEO for about ten minutes, and then if you think it has merit I can meet with someone else. (Without pause) Would 9:00 or 11:00 on Tuesday work for you?" (Alternate of choice)

"A stumbling voice gathers no appointment."

The key to answering phone objections during the approach is to be confident and know what you're going to say. A stumbling voice gathers no appointment. No matter what I sold, I had canned phone approaches, and I practiced it in training repeatedly before I turned rookie salespeople loose.

My first summer selling books, I had trouble getting into houses the first week. When I showed my manager my approach at the end of that first week, he said, "No wonder you're not getting in; you're saying way too much."

Here's what he taught me: "Hello, Mrs. Carter, my name is Tom Black. I've just been out in the neighborhood calling on all the families with children. May I come in?"

I know why it worked. The simplicity and directness were critical. I expected to come in, and they sensed that. When they objected, I was prepared and gave the answer I mentioned before. The second key is to remember the approach is your way of getting permission to give a presentation, not to give the presentation. Here is a general rule of thumb to keep in mind about the approach: The less said the better.

In Review

- Most people have buying rituals, which can appear to be real objections, so treat them like real objections and see them as practice for the really tough ones.

- When dealing with the unspoken objection, you must invite the objection through a very direct question that gets you to the truth behind the prospect's hesitation.

- When it comes to answering any objection, you must first isolate it. When you do this, you can more easily address it and overcome it.

- For the two types of price objections, "I can't afford it", and "Your price is higher than the competitor", the more direct your approach to this the better.

- You will hear objections in the approach. You can't ignore them, but don't lose momentum.

- Remember that the phone approach is designed to get the appointment, not sell the product.

- The key to answering phone objections during the approach is to be confident and know what you're going to say.

Chapter 20

The Science of the Follow-Up

Most salespeople don't close their sale on the first call. However, I believe it is possible to close every sale on the first call if all of the decision makers are there.

In the book business, that meant either the husband or the wife. Both could make the decision I was asking for, and there was never any follow-up.

On the other hand, the ten different programs we sold to banks sometimes required follow-up. So we developed some pretty specific strategies for our follow-up. These strategies can be applied to any kind of sales that require follow-up.

"The cold call follow-up is a last resort."

The Follow-Up: Part of Your Sales Talk

First of all, follow-up is always set up in the last call – either in person, by email, by snail mail, or on the phone. Your follow-up should be designed with a specific expectation of results. The cold call follow-up is a last resort. It can be used, but the best follow-up is planned with the prospect fully aware when you are following up, and more importantly, what your expectations are for the meeting.

Here is a specific example of what I'm talking about. You call on a prospect for the first time. You make your presentation, you close, you answer objections, and you discover there are other decision-makers and influencers you must meet with.

So you say something like this: "Mr. Jackson, what I'd like to do is set up a meeting with the other people involved in the decision making process. Could we meet today or later this week?"

The prospect says, "yes", and you continue: "What I'd like to do at that meeting is explain the program and answer any questions the group may have. Then if it seems appropriate, you can let me know whether you want to move forward. Does that sound fair?"

Strike While the Iron is Hot

Now let's dissect what I just said. First, I tried to set up the next meeting ASAP. The quicker the follow-up, the more momentum you have to keep moving forward. Second, the quicker the follow-up, the less chance for new objections, competitors, or hurricanes to come along. I am annoyed by the lack of a sense of urgency in salespeople when following up. For every day that goes by between one call and the next, the chances of making the sale go down.

Can you imagine a boy taking a girl home from a date, walking her up to the door and saying, "I'll be back in a few days for my kiss"?

Selling and courting have a lot in common, and both suffer from a lack of contact and a slowing of momentum.

It's a little late to call Mr. Edwards back now, isn't it?

After I've asked permission for the follow-up and it's given, I tell the prospect what to expect from the next meeting. We're going to all be together – including the prospect – at which point I'll answer questions, and at the end of the meeting

I'll be expecting a decision.

Finally, I get agreement by asking, "Does that sound fair?"

This is a very powerful question. No one wants to be unfair. So this question will always get a "yes" if indeed your proposition is fair.

Confirmation is Crucial

The next step in the follow-up is a confirmation of the meeting. Many salespeople don't do this. They haven't ever been told to do it, they put it off, or they simply forget. This one thing will give you ten to twenty percent more effective follow-up meetings and improve your time utilization as well.

So now that the second meeting is set, send an email to the prospect immediately. In the email, confirm the date, time, and who you expect to be in attendance. In addition, give a brief agenda. For example, the agenda should be succinct and to-the-point like this:

1. We will discuss the details of the program (product, service, etc).
2. I will answer questions the group has.
3. We will talk about the implementation schedule.
4. We'll determine who will be named program director.
5. We will discuss the contract.

My agenda is made up of the things every prospect must do before they buy. So here is a good time to insert this idea. There are certain things in every sale that prospects do before they buy. These things are: Read the contract, pick a program director, schedule training, involve other people, and so on.

Every product that is sold has its own set of events or actions that a prospect must go through before the purchase decision is made. This is a good list for every salesperson to make; it will help you identify whether a prospect is moving toward a sale or not.

Now you've sent the email confirming the appointment – and the prospect knows you're serious. Unless the appointment is the next day, give the prospect a call to confirm your appointment. That call, if you actually get to speak to your prospect and not his voicemail, should confirm the appointment. It also serves to test the water if you add a question like, "Have you had any questions come up since we met?"

If you have to leave a message, then just confirm the appointment. This three-step approach to follow-up is the best one I've found.

Here are some rules to follow about follow-up meetings. First, don't go see the prospect again unless you can actually move the sale forward. Second, don't follow up with a drop-in unless it's absolutely necessary. Unexpected drop-ins are a last resort. Third, always set your expectations for follow-ups with the prospects. It makes meetings much more productive. Fourth, always confirm the meeting by phone if the follow-up is more than one day away.

In Review

- Set follow-ups during the last call.

- Follow-ups should be designed with a specific expectation of results.

- Set up the next meeting as soon as possible for two reasons: First, the quicker the follow-up, the more momentum you have to keep moving forward. And second, this gives less time for new objections to come along.

- Get confirmation of the follow-up meeting. Confirm the date, time, who you expect to be in attendance, and give a brief agenda.

- Unless the appointment is the next day, give the prospect a call to confirm your appointment.

- Don't go see the prospect again unless you can actually move the sale forward.

- Don't follow up with a drop-in unless it's absolutely necessary.

Chapter 21

The Not-So-Immediate Follow-Up

"You need to keep as much sales momentum as possible..."

Keeping them on the Roller Coaster

Now let's assume the follow-up meeting is not so immediate – that there is a longer period of time between the first meeting and the second. But you need to keep as much sales momentum as possible, so how do you do this? Here are some ideas that have worked. Emails or snail-mail letters are good – it's never a bad idea to use a follow-up letter. I have several canned follow-up letters that can be sent out almost automatically.

Here's an example:

> *Dear Mr. Jackson,*
>
> *It was nice meeting you today. Hopefully it will be the beginning of a longer relationship. It was interesting to hear about your involvement with the Boy Scouts and United Way.*
>
> *I believe our program can help you in three ways: (Fill in the Blanks with strong benefits you noticed caught the prospect's attention).*
>
> *I'll look forward to seeing you in two weeks, September 15th, at 9 a.m.*
>
> *All the Best,*
>
> *Tom Black*

So, why do a letter like this? First, only one in a hundred salespeople actually do it, so you differentiate yourself. Second, this reinforces your visit and the benefits of your program, service, or product. Third, you're beginning to build a relationship – as you can see in the letter, I mentioned something the prospect and I had talked about personally.

"Differentiate yourself..."

A second idea to keep your sales momentum going between the first and second meeting is a letter or email from your superior. We used a letter from the President or CEO. It was a canned letter and was sent automatically when we requested it. The letter was yet another way for us to differentiate ourselves from the competition and keep that ever-important sales momentum going. How many prospects get a letter from the president of a company before they buy? The letter should be short – two paragraphs are plenty.

Ours went something like this:

> *Dear Mr. Jackson,*
>
> *Tom Black, our sales representative in Kansas, said he met with you recently. Hopefully you enjoyed his visit. We're very excited about the potential of your company using our product (service, program, etc).*
>
> *Our product has been shown to.... (Include several strong benefits here).*
>
> *If I can answer any questions or concerns, feel free to call me at 615-555-1212 or email me at president@bmc.com.*
>
> *Sincerely yours,*
>
> *Ima Bigshot*

Throughout my career in sales, these letters have been well received and also well read by prospects, so make sure you sell what is most important in the benefits paragraph of the letter. And, keep it short . . . one page at the most.

Just Look at all these Happy Customers!

A third idea for maintaining momentum between meetings is to communicate good news. If someone new buys your product, it's a good idea to share this with your follow-up prospect by phone or email. You can also communicate current customers' success stories about your product. Let your prospect hear that someone they know (if possible) is having success with your product, service, or program. This third party success story is a great way to ensure you keep your momentum into the next meeting.

Almost anything you can think of to keep you in the prospect's mind during that break between meetings is good. Notice I said almost anything. I wouldn't recommend stalking. But you do have many legal ways to keep communication going to keep you fresh in the prospect's mind. In addition to in-person visits, you have the phone, email, and snail mail at your disposal, in addition to other people contacting your prospect.

"Don't push hard and then not deliver."

I never went through rush in college, but that's how I imagine the process is between the first and second visits. I do have one caveat: Don't push hard and then not deliver. If you decide to put on the "rush" between the first and second visit, then be sure you can deliver.

A man died and went to see St. Peter. St. Peter said, "You have a choice between Heaven and Hell – to help you decide, you'll spend one week in Heaven and one in Hell. At the end of the two weeks, you'll choose where you'll spend eternity."

First, the man spent his week in Hell, and it was a week filled with wine, women, and song. He spent his week in Heaven, and it was everything he thought it would be.

However, he felt more comfortable in Hell, so he told St. Peter, "I choose Hell."

Well, poof! He was in an inferno being whipped and tortured by demons. He cried out, "Hey wait a minute! Last week I was here, and it was nothing like this!"

The Devil spoke up and said, "Well, of course not! Last week you were a prospect. This week you're a customer!"

If you make a promise, deliver on it. Under-promise and over-deliver. There is no other standard.

Oh, no, no, I wasn't lying! That was just creative selling.

So at this point, you've made contact with your prospect by email, phone, and mail. You've showed them new buyers and shared success stories with your prospect, and now you're ready for your second meeting. You've confirmed the meeting and set expectations. The stage is set.

Here are a couple of thoughts on the second meeting that are important to remember. If all the decision makers are there, then get a decision. Second, be prepared to close at the end of the meeting. If you've set it up properly and set expectations, then closing is a real possibility. Third, remember that a "no" doesn't equal a "no sale".

Particularly in a group meeting, one negative person is just that – negative. Many times that negative person will sell the others. Fourth, be ready to excuse yourself from the meeting and let them decide.

That close should sound like this: "Mr. Jackson, since all the decision makers are here, I'd like to step out and let you all discuss this program and decide whether or not you would like to move forward. Does that sound fair?"

"Excuse yourself, don't wait for an answer, and you'll get your answer."

Remember that a "no" is better than a stall. You did your job and you got a decision. This close works. Sometimes the answer isn't what you want, but it is an answer and lets you move on. The group will never make a better decision than immediately after your presentation when they are all together and focused on your product.

The biggest mistake and the one I've seen most often in regard to follow-ups is a lack of urgency about keeping the momentum going. Every day that goes by after an initial presentation, the prospect loses some of their initial enthusiasm. The second mistake I see is a lack of creativity in follow-ups. A call simply to say, "Have you made your decision yet?" is a waste when you can be adding additional positive information. Finally, most salespeople don't use their company resources. Calls or letters from other company members are both impressive and effective. The use of letters and emails should be a habit and closing after a meeting with all decision makers, a must.

In Review

• Here are three ways to keep as much sales momentum as possible during the time between your last call and a not-so-immediate follow up:

 1. Use a follow-up letter. This differentiates you from other sales people, reinforces your visit and the benefits of your program, service, or product, and further builds a relationship.
 2. Use a one-page letter or email from your superior.
 3. Communicate good news. Let your prospect hear a third party success story about your product, service, or program.

• Always under promise and over deliver.

• Here are some thoughts to remember for the second meeting:

 1. If all the decision makers are there, get a decision.
 2. Be prepared to close at the end of the meeting.
 3. Remember that a "no" doesn't equal a "no sale".

"If you cannot see someone who can say 'yes',
your time is better spent going
somewhere else."

Chapter 22

The Hunt for the Elusive Quality Prospect

Now it's time to move to the third factor that determines results in selling: The quality of the prospect. It goes without saying that the best presentation in the world and the hardest working salesperson can still improve by improving the quality of prospects that they see.

This first became evident to me in the book business. When I started out, I went to every house. Soon I learned the best prospects have jobs and children. I talked to lots of people my first summer who didn't have kids. Since most of the books I sold were for families, that just didn't make sense. Some young couples without kids bought, and a few older couples bought for their grandkids, but the higher percentages of my sales were from families with jobs. So when I went to only those families and passed on others, my sales almost doubled.

Basketball coaches know this principle; that's why they don't let their players shoot half-court shots. A lay-up is easy, but you have to fight to get to the basket.

Football coaches know this, so they don't call Hail Marys on every play. Long shots are just that – long shots. As they say, "The exception proves the rule."

Go Where There is Power, Or Don't Go At All

The first product we sold to banks had a marketing element to it. So, the President or CEO would always say, "You need to see the marketing director."

"If we couldn't see the CEO, we just didn't go..."

When we were weak and actually did that, we rarely made the sale. The marketing directors didn't have the authority to say "yes." The only answers we got from marketing directors were "maybe" or "no." This happened so universally that we made a rule: If we couldn't see the CEO, we just didn't go (it rhymes).

Once we made this rule, everyone got better at selling the decision makers. If you cannot see someone who can say 'yes', your time is better spent going somewhere else. The hard part about this isn't in understanding the theory. It is in implementing it.

I have a friend who is a drug rep. Her attitude is that anyone is better than no one. But the doctor is the only one prescribing drugs, and giving the sales presentation to anyone else is simply not effective. She won't fight to get to the basket. You can make yourself do this.

Escape the Rut

There was a night watchman that got off at midnight every night. His path home took him through a cemetery, and week after week he would walk home through this cemetery. One night the cemetery crew left an open grave, and on the night watchman's way home, he fell in. He tried and tried to get out but couldn't, so he settled into a dark corner to wait for the grave digging crew to return in the morning.

Another man was walking down the path a few minutes later and the same thing happened. He fell into the open grave.

The night watchman, hidden in his dark corner, was amused to see the new man try the same methods he had to escape the pit. After a few minutes of watching him struggle, he said from the darkness, "You can't get out of here." But the second man did.

"...a rut is just a grave with the ends knocked out."

Well if you're seeing decision-makers 100 percent of the time, you can get out of that rut. Remember in sales, a rut is just a grave with the ends knocked out.

No matter what you're selling, it is hard to see decision-makers every time because there are so many gatekeepers. But look at it this way: If they are that hard to see, that likely is their point of resistance in the sales process.

Once you get past this, the road is easier. Steep resistance to sales calls is like a sign that says, "Hunt here! Plenty of quail!"

No other salespeople are seeing them either.

Quality Knows Quality

Part of gaining more quality prospects is getting referrals from other qualified prospects. Here is a method I like – I try to do this technique in person first, but I've also done it by both phone and email. As I am speaking to a satisfied customer or a new buyer (someone who can also serve as a referral) I say:

"Mr. Jackson, as you know, I'm looking for other people in this industry that might want to use our product. (Notice I didn't say "interested in" here.) Do any other bankers come to mind that I should call on?"

I expect a "no, not really" response. When I get a banker that gives me referrals, that's a bonus . . . and now my work really starts.

Let's assume you get the expected "no, not really" response. Your question to that response should be: "How about somebody in your peer group?"

"Peer group" is a banking term, but you can use any group that people in which your customer's industry are members or participate in. This may remind the customer of a few people and he'll provide a name or two or more.

> *"Help your referral sources think of other people they know."*

Ticklers

If I still haven't gotten a few names from this customer, I keep using what I call "ticklers". Ticklers are spheres of influence that my customer might have. Remember the prospect list? If all else fails, I pull out my prospect list and ask if he knows some of the bankers I will be calling on. If he does, then I try to get a referral that way. In any case, the key to getting referrals is by helping your referral sources think of other people they know. It takes practice like everything else in sales.

Have Them Do Your Approach

The strongest kind of referral is when the referral source makes an initial contact for you. You can use a statement like this: "It would help, Mr. Jackson, if you could just drop Mr. Stevens an email and let him know I'll be calling him."

If you can get your satisfied customer to do this, it's better than saying something like: "Mr. Jackson suggested I call you."

This too takes practice, and you will face some rejection when you ask, but you should still ask every referral source to do this to help you.

Well sir, you're right, there is no door to Mr. Jones' office. Good luck - you'll need it.

Fight for the Best

So you have a great prospect based on what you know. Maybe it's based on a referral from someone or maybe it's based on your own information. In any case, you can get creative in your approach. Remember you can secure your appointment in person, over the phone, by third party, via email, and through snail mail. If one doesn't work, try another.

When I have a prospect I really want to see, and my first approach (typically by phone) is rejected, then I have other methods as well. Very few salespeople – usually only the great ones – try other methods after the first one fails. Strive to be one of these great salespeople. Write an email, send a proposal letter, or go call on the prospect in person.

Many salespeople don't fight to see the qualified prospect because as we all know, it's easier to see someone who wants to see us. I've actually heard salespeople say, "I needed to get my presentations/demos up, so I went to see those prospects I knew couldn't say "yes."

I wish they could hear themselves. I've had arguments with salespeople who say, "But Tom! I had a prospect this one time who bought and wasn't the decision maker."

My response: "OK, how much time did you waste with other non-decision makers to get that one little exception?"

Don't resist the rules of the game, play by them and you'll win.

By the same token I've heard it the other way, too. Like this: "Well, my presentations are low because I only want to talk to qualified prospects."

Well you can't do that! Remember at the beginning of the book that was an excuse given by one of my salespeople, and then two other salespeople in her organization beat her by doing both – seeing lots of people and making sure they were qualified prospects.

There is just no escaping the fact that the best of all worlds is qualified prospects seen lots of times with polished presentation skills.

In Review

- The third factor in the "sales saga" is the quality of the prospects you see.

- Find the decision makers – if you cannot see someone who can say 'yes', your time is better spent going somewhere else.

- Other qualified prospects are an excellent referral source for gaining more quality prospects.

- Use "tickers", the spheres of influence that my customer might have.

- The strongest kind of referral is when the referral source makes an initial contact for you.

- Stop making excuses and fight for the best appointments.

Now you know most of what I know about selling. It's simple, and it's hard. You've got to see more people, give great presentations, and do it all with qualified prospects

You also know now how to get yourself out of a sales slump. Like a doctor diagnosing a patient, you can diagnose your own slump. Slumps are either caused by the number of presentations you are giving, the quality of those presentations, or the quality of your prospects.

It's really that simple, and you've got the details for the diagnosis behind you.

Chapter

The Critical Role of Ethics

My Selling System is Not Successful Without the Role of Ethics

Ethics is a big word; we could discuss its role in sales and in life for hours, days, or weeks, but for now I want to share with you a little about ethics' key role in the world of professional selling. There are certain rules of fair play in selling and most can be summed up in a single word: Honesty.

There are endless chances in selling to be dishonest. Sometimes you will never get caught, but for most of us, the stress and tension of living with a lie is just as bad as getting caught. Teddy Roosevelt once said, "Character in the long run is the decisive factor in the life of an individual and of nations alike."

Honesty to Self

The first place you must practice honesty is with yourself. Polonius, in Shakespeare's *Hamlet*, says, "This above all, to thine own self be true, and it must follow as the night the day. Thou canst not then be false to any man."

"Honesty to ourselves is the key to honesty with others."

Most of the time, if we look in our heart of hearts, we know what do to. The real hope of improvement and happiness lie in the acceptance of who we are – both strengths and weaknesses alike. And then striving to improve on the weaknesses and make the strengths grow stronger. Honesty to ourselves is the key to honesty with others.

One Saturday afternoon, a preacher was preparing his sermon in his study. His four-year-old son kept bothering him, and so to keep him busy, he tore a page from a magazine with a map of the world on it. He tore the map into little pieces to make a puzzle for his son. He gave the pieces to the boy thinking that it would keep his son busy for hours. Instead, a few minutes later, the boy returned with the map in perfect order.

"How did you put it together so quickly?" the preacher asked his son.

"When you ripped out the page from the magazine," said the boy, "I noticed a man on the backside of the map. I knew if I put the man together right, the world would be right."

Truer words were never spoken.

Here is a poem that I think sums up this idea of honesty to oneself. It is called "The Man in the Glass":

> *When you get what you want in the struggle for self,*
> *And the world makes you King for a Day;*
> *Just go to a mirror and look at yourself,*
> *And see what that man has to say.*
> *For it isn't your father or mother or wife,*
> *Whose judgment upon you must pass;*
> *The fellow whose verdict counts most in your life,*
> *Is the one staring back from the glass.*
> *Some people may think you're a straight-shootin' chum,*
> *And call you a wonderful guy;*
> *But the man in the glass says you're only a bum,*
> *If you can't look him straight in the eye.*
> *He's the fellow to please, never mind all the rest,*
> *For he's with you clear up to the end;*
> *And you've passed your most dangerous, difficult test,*
> *If the man in the glass is your friend.*
> *You may fool the whole world down the pathway of life,*
> *And get pats on the back as you pass;*
> *But your final reward will be heartaches and tears,*
> *If you've cheated the man in the glass.*

Honesty to Your Prospects

The second obligation we have is to be honest with our prospects. It's always better to tell the truth than try to remember a lie. Intuitively, a high percentage of prospects can detect when they are being misled.

Here are a few basic guidelines to abide by when dealing with prospects and customers:

- Don't overstate the benefits of your product.
- Don't leave details out purposely that will hurt your prospect.
- Don't accept money under false pretenses.
- Don't offer money under false pretenses.

Benjamin Franklin said, "Honesty is the best policy. A person who isn't honest just doesn't have the sense God gave a goose." In the long run, good guys do win.

> ## *"No long term success will ever come from anything but honesty."*

I learned early in my career to be honest with my prospects. Once when I was selling books, I used the name of a person who I had talked to but hadn't bought from me. The prospect confronted me, and I lost that sale and all the others that were in the prospect's sphere of influence. In the banking world, I saw the same kind of thing. No long term success will ever come from anything but honesty.

When a bank prospect called one of my current customers, the best thing those customers could say was, "You can count on them, me, or the company (they were all the same) to do what he says."

In my opinion, there can be no better recommendation.

There is no salesperson who can call himself a salesperson who can't look a customer in the eye and feel good about the transaction.

In one company I am chairman of, we fix ATMs. We often buy used ATMs, and in one used ATM, we discovered $80,000 inside that clearly did not belong to us.

Finders Keepers? Not really. We spent $5000 in legal fees trying to figure out whose money it was, and when we did, we sent all $80,000 back. Too many salespeople and companies I know would have abided by the *Finders Keepers* mentality.

Bottom line: It just wasn't our money. As salespeople this is the attitude we must have. Look for a fair deal for the prospect in addition to a fair deal for you and your company.

The Government and I disagreed on what ethics are exactly.

Honesty to Your Company

The third place where honesty must be present is with your company. Your company is like a ship; all the employees are on board. Well, you can't sink half of a ship. If the crew goes down, the officers go down as well. Ultimately, everyone benefits or doesn't benefit together.

What does this mean to you? It means that you should never lie or stretch your numbers on a sales activity report. Either you made the calls or you didn't. Either way, just be a man or a woman about it and face up to your performance. Never fudge an expense report. Sure, you can pick up an extra hundred dollars or so a week by doing it, but the risk is not worth it, and the poison it puts in your own system is definitely not worth it.

Remember, whatever you put in the lives of others comes back into your own.

Over the years I've worked with lots of "fighter pilot" salespeople. They might as well have starred in *Top Gun*. They were only out for themselves.

The attitude of these salespeople was one of, "Why should I do anything to help the company if I don't get paid for it?"

Perhaps that is not technically dishonest, but it's as close as you can get.

If there's a hole in the boat, and you don't plug it when you can, then that's worse than dishonest. It's just plain dumb. If you cash a man's check, then you support what he does, and when you can't support it, it's time to get another job.

I've actually had salespeople working for one of my companies try to recruit other salespeople in our company to go to a competitor with them when they decided to leave – and they did it while they were still on my payroll. As the redneck comedian Jeff Foxworthy says, "That ain't right."

It is a truth that so many people are interested in getting all that is coming to them, and not in giving more than they get. People who just do the job don't get promoted.

People who overflow the job get more money and more responsibility.

So, when it comes to sales ethics, honesty just about sums it up, but here is another thought. Whether it's honesty or something else, you can't buy business – the long-term and profitable kind we all want – with anything but good service and good products.

Bribes, sexual favors, and inappropriate gifts are all short-term quick fixes to long-term problems; and they just flat don't work.

Got Code?

Does your company have a code of ethics?

If it doesn't, I suggest that you write one for them. Go online and find one you like, and then you can adapt it to your company. Every company should have a written code of ethics.

Another question for you: If you do work for a business that has a code, does your company give only a single training session or more than one on this code of ethics? Is it even discussed at all? If not, suggest they start.

Remember what words come to mind when most people think of a salesperson:

Pushy, high pressure, conman, charlatan, cheat, dishonest, twists your arm, makes you buy.

Each one of us as salespeople must do our part to change this image. I've heard that an "ethical salesperson" is an oxymoron. Let's start changing that formally. Here is the Rotary International Code of Ethics; they call it "The Four Way Test". It's short, simplistic, straight shooting, and is a good place to start if you want to write your own:

> Of the things we think, say, or do:
>
> 1.Is it the TRUTH?
> 2.Is it FAIR to all concerned?
> 3.Will it build GOODWILL and BETTER FRIENDSHIPS?
> 4.Will it be BENEFICIAL to all concerned?

Now, you can teach a code of ethics to salespeople. You can give them a test, and in an artificial atmosphere, most everyone would get all the expected answers right. You can even improve behavior and acceptance of an ethical standard with punitive measures. You can even reward ethical behavior.

However, the best way to be ethical is to live by your own personal code of ethics. Every study, book, or great manager I know say this is accomplished best by a meaningful religious conviction.

I am not here to preach. My goal is to give helpful advice and formulas for success. Over and over again I am confronted with the fact that we as human beings don't have enough emotional will power to overcome the obstacles of life without this connection to a higher power. If I didn't believe that, I'd hate to compete against the man or woman who did. I believe with all my heart that this meaningful religious conviction is a connection to unlimited power far beyond what any of us have in our own little battery packs.

"Selling can become a calling that lifts you up."

When you involve a personal code of ethics with a relationship to a higher power, you can be more than successful in your career. Your career can actually lift you up and give you purpose. Selling can become a calling that lifts you up.

Man is not made in a crisis. He is revealed in the crisis. If you're going to stand up in the storm, you ought to know how you're anchored.

Doing Nothing: The Worst Kind of Action

One final question for you on ethics: What do you do if the company you work for is not ethical according to your personal standards?

If they're breaking the law, you should call the district attorney, the police, or your own attorney. The point is to report them.

No matter what your current economic situation, it can only get worse by working for a company that is breaking the law. You must make your own decision. In the long run, a company that endorses dishonesty at any level will ultimately fail. When it fails, you shouldn't be working there.

When I interview salespeople and they tell me they left their previous company because it was unethical, I can't remember one of those salespeople who ever did anything about it.

When I ask them, "So what did you do about it?" their response is, "I left."

Well that's all well and good, but I think more is required than just leaving. Let's get on the record somewhere – the CEO, the authorities, the other salespeople – tell someone that you can't work in a company that is dishonest.

Somehow our value system has become this: If I know about something dishonest that is going on, but I don't participate, this gives me a free pass.

I say "horse hockey" to that.

> *"Situation ethics are no ethics at all."*

There was a fraternity at Duke University that dropped a pledge off in the country with no clothes, only the very realistic Blue Devils mascot costume. Having nothing else to wear, the pledge put on the costume and started walking back to the university. It started raining, and in an attempt to avoid getting in trouble with his fraternity by ruining the costume, the pledge decided to look for shelter.

The first thing he saw was a little country church. Inside the church, the preacher really had the congregation worked up. He was stomping and yelling, and the congregation was giving him an "amen" after every sentence.

Now, the pledge thought he would just slip into the waiting area of the church until it stopped raining. When he opened the door, however, he was standing right behind the preacher. This caused quite a stir. People started jumping up and out the windows, out the back door, and one rather large woman decided to go out the door the Blue Devil had entered.

Well, the Blue Devil had the same idea at the same time, and the two of them got stuck in the doorway. Very quickly, the woman said, "Between you and me, Mr. Devil, I been on your side all along."

Well, situation ethics are no ethics at all.

In scouting I was always told, "Integrity is what you do when no one's there to watch or tell you what to do."

You don't get a free pass if you know the company is doing something wrong and you just leave. If my neighbor was being robbed, I wouldn't pull down the shades. If another neighbor was beating his wife, I wouldn't just turn up the volume on the TV. And if my co-workers, my customers, or my friends were not being treated ethically, I'd try to solve it the best way I could within my means.

If

When I graduated from high school my Aunt Pauline gave me a poem I carried in my wallet and read every day in college; and it now hangs in my bathroom at home. It's called "If" by Rudyard Kipling, and it's my personal code of ethics:

> *If you can keep your head when all about you*
> *Are losing theirs and blaming it on you,*
> *If you can trust yourself when all men doubt you*
> *But make allowance for their doubting too,*
> *If you can wait and not be tired by waiting,*
> *Or being lied about, don't deal in lies,*

Or being hated, don't give way to hating,
And yet don't look too good, nor talk too wise:
If you can dream – and not make dreams your master,
If you can think – and not make thoughts your aim;
If you can meet with Triumph and Disaster
And treat those two impostors just the same;
If you can bear to hear the truth you've spoken
Twisted by knaves to make a trap for fools,
Or watch the things you gave your life to, broken,
And stoop and build 'em up with worn-out tools:
If you can make one heap of all your winnings
And risk it on one turn of pitch-and-toss,
And lose, and start again at your beginnings
And never breath a word about your loss;
If you can force your heart and nerve and sinew
To serve your turn long after they are gone,
And so hold on when there is nothing in you
Except the Will which says to them: "Hold on!"
If you can talk with crowds and keep your virtue,
Or walk with kings – nor lose the common touch,
If neither foes nor loving friends can hurt you;
If all men count with you, but none too much,
If you can fill the unforgiving minute
With sixty seconds' worth of distance run,
Yours is the Earth and everything that's in it,
And – which is more – you'll be a Man, my son!

In Review

• Ethics is a matter of honesty: Honesty to yourself, your prospects, and your company.

• Develop your own personal code of ethics by which to live and work.

• Commit to a higher power.

• The "don't tell" policy of reporting ethical behavior doesn't work. In some cases, inaction in ethical matters is just as bad as the act itself.

"It's our job as salespeople to make sure this 'sandbox' of ours gets passed on for future generations to play in."

Chapter 24

The Sandbox that is America

Welcome To Our Sandbox

This final chapter is about what I call the "sandbox", which allows all of us to operate as salespeople: The American System.

By the American System, I am referring to the free enterprise system of fair competition and the governmental and legal system that guarantees our individual, inalienable rights. Can you imagine selling in North Korea, where none of these elements of our "sandbox" exists?

I gave a speech at my alma mater, and the subject was, "What I Fear as a Baby Boomer." Personally, it isn't the failure of the Social Security system, a fear of Medicare failure, experiencing nuclear war, or battling terrorists. My fear is that we aren't passing along the system, the values of the "sandbox".

I coached a high school debate team for eight years, and one day one of the kids asked me, "How do you feel about America?"

My response, in keeping with my style with anyone I am trying to teach, was, "Well, Mike, how do you feel about America?"

Mike said he didn't know. He didn't feel that he loved America and he didn't know why people said they did.

I explained that, in America, there is unlimited opportunity. Our system isn't perfect, but our system is the best in the world for maximizing the human potential. I also said that America is the only hope for the rest of the world for freedom to survive. I told Mike that sometimes individuals can make us doubt our system, but those individuals are so rare, they prove the rule.

I told him that it is OK to be patriotic, that citizenship is a gift our forefathers gave us, and that lots of men and women died to preserve our rights. I also explained there was nothing wrong with the word "patriotism" and that it was an obligation of "citizenship."

"The American System allows you to get paid what you are worth..."

I told him that the promise of America is the pursuit of happiness and self-actualization. The American System allows you to get paid what you are worth, not what some group says an individual deserves or votes for instead of earns.

The Systems Still Works

Right now, we find ourselves frustrated as Americans. I've been frustrated three times in my life as an American: Vietnam, President Nixon's behavior, and the war in Iraq. Well, we as Americans like "straight forward." We like to win and we like to know who the enemy is. We also like to keep score and always know the score. Now we're on the defensive. We are reacting; we can't get the ball. The better team doesn't seem to be winning.

Just like the three times in history during my life, events can go against the things we like as Americans, and so we become frustrated. However, the system is still working. Individual achievement, economically and personally, grows higher every year with very few dips. More people have jobs and are making more money than ever before.

It is like the scientist who trained the flea to jump out of the jar. He told the flea to "jump", and out the flea jumped. He then took off one of the flea's pairs of legs and told the flea to "jump" the flea was still able to jump out of the jar.

He removed a second pair of legs and said "jump," and the flea made the jump out of the jar yet again. When he removed the final set and said "jump," the flea couldn't jump at all.

Here was the scientist's conclusion: "When you remove the legs of a flea, it becomes deaf."

It's the wrong conclusion – just because we're frustrated or uneducated doesn't mean the system doesn't work. That is a wrong conclusion, too.

Just Do Your Part

It's our job as salespeople to make sure this "sandbox" of ours gets passed on for future generations to play in. We should be selling America every chance we get.

We shouldn't let people believe it is their right to vote themselves benefits from the public coffers, or that a good congressman is one who gets the most benefits for his district, or even that a tax refund is a government benefit, "It was your money to start with!"

Surely there is someone else we can blame for this.

Believe me, I am not preaching politics here, just principles that allow salespeople to make as much money as they can and to rise up as high economically as they can. Each of us has a little piece of America to protect. Truth is not self-evident. It must be told and revealed.

You can make a child just as good a Socialist or Communist with instruction as you can an American. There is nothing about being born in America that guarantees a value system that believes in and promotes free enterprise. It's part of our job as salespeople to sell that system.

James Agee, a Pulitzer prize winning author, said, "In every child born, under no matter what circumstances, and of no matter what parents, the potentiality of the human race is born again. And in him, too, once more, and of each of us, our terrific responsibility toward human life; toward the utmost ideals of goodness, of the horror of terror, and of God."

I heard a poem as a student, a Poem entitled *"Education"* by Arthur Guiterman. Williams College bases their educational philosophy on this poem:

> *Mark Hopkins sat on one end of a log,*
> *And a farm boy sat on the other.*
> *Mark Hopkins came as a pedagogue*
> *And taught as an elder brother.*
> *I don't care what Mark Hopkins taught,*
> *If his Latin was small and his Greek was naught,*
> *For the farmer boy he thought, thought he,*
> *All through lecture time and quiz,*
> *'The kind of man I mean to be,*
> *Is the kind of a man Mark Hopkins is!'*
> *...For education is making men!*
> *So is it now, so was it when*
> *Mark Hopkins sat on one end of a log,*
> *And James Garfield sat on the other.*

The farm boy in the poem was James Garfield, one of the Garfield kids, who became president of the United States.

As salespeople we can't continue to assume that the next generation will support the sandbox in which we play. I think it was Longfellow who said, "One man can awaken another, and two can awaken a third, and three can wake a village, and a village can awaken a nation."

In addition to everything else, let's do our part to ensure that we pass this system on, too. Margaret Mead said, "Never doubt that a small group of thoughtful, committed citizens can change the world. Indeed, it is the only thing that ever has."

Parents may struggle to pay for education, special training camps, or tutors, but most will never spend a dime or a minute on basic American values.

There is a story well known to everyone, the story of The *Ugly Duckling*. Although it is passed off many times as a simple children's tale, the duckling's story embodies the most fundamental ideals of the American System:

Then he felt quite ashamed, and hid his head under his wing; for he did not know what to do, he was so happy, and yet not at all proud. He had been persecuted and despised for his ugliness, and now he heard them say he was the most beautiful of all the birds. The sun shone warm and bright. Then he rustled his feathers, curved his slender neck, and cried joyfully, from the depths of his heart, "I never dreamed of such happiness as this, while I was an ugly duckling."

The duckling never dreamed of the kind of beauty that he could possess. But as Americans, we are all capable of finding that beauty, that success, or anything else we strive for. That is what makes the American System unlike any other in the world.

"Let's strive to keep America a place where a kid can start in a boxcar, start with nothing and end up the CEO of a public company and living in a mansion."

Notes

Notes

Notes